The Promise of Productive Aging

Robert N. Butler, M.D., is Brookdale Professor and Chairman of The Gerald and May Ellen Ritter Department of Geriatrics and Adult Development at the Mount Sinai School of Medicine in New York City, the nation's first medical school department of geriatrics. Dr. Butler was founding director of the National Institute on Aging (1975–1982). In 1976 he won the Pulitzer Prize for his book *Why Survive? Being Old in America*. Dr. Butler is editor-in-chief of the journal *Geriatrics*, chairs programs for the Commonwealth and Brookdale foundations, served on the U.S. Congress Physicians Payment Review Commission, and sits on the boards of many of the country's leading associations.

Mia R. Oberlink is a writer and editor specializing in issues related to aging. Since joining The Gerald and May Ellen Ritter Department of Geriatrics and Adult Development in 1986 she has been writing for professional, academic, and lay audiences on a wide range of topics in the field, from government policy to human aging research.

Mal Schechter is assistant professor of geriatrics and adult development in The Gerald and May Ellen Ritter Department of Geriatrics and Adult Development. From 1960 to 1979 he was a medical and political writer in Washington, D.C., specializing in population aging issues. Thereafter he served as an expert consultant to the National Institute on Aging until 1982. He is co-author of *Aging 2000: A Challenge to Society* (MTP Press, 1981).

The Promise of Productive Aging: From Biology to Social Policy

Robert N. Butler, M.D.
Mia R. Oberlink
Mal Schechter

Editors

Based on a symposium held in Washington, DC,
April 28–29, 1987

Springer Publishing Company
New York

Springer Publishing Company, Inc.
536 Broadway
New York, NY 10012

90 91 92 93 94 / 5 4 3 2 1

Library of Congress Cataloging-in-Publication Data

The Promise of productive aging : from biology to social policy /
  Robert N. Butler, Mia R. Oberlink, Mal Schechter, editors.
     p.   cm.
  "Based on a symposium held in Washington, DC, April 28–29, 1987."
  Includes bibliographical references.
  ISBN 0-8261-6270-3 : $28.95 (32.50 foreign)
  1. Aged—Congresses. 2. Aging—Congresses. 3. Age and
employment—Congresses. 4. Aged—Government policy—Congresses.
I. Butler, Robert N., 1927–   . II. Oberlink, Mia R.
III. Schechter, Mal.
  IDNLM: 1. Aged—congresses. 2. Aging—congresses. 3. Efficiency-
-in old age—congresses. 4. Employment—congresses. WT 100 P965
1967]
HC:061.P785 1990
305.26—dc20
DNLM/DLC
for Library of Congress   89-26375
                                            CIP

Printed in the United States of America

Contents

Chapter 12. Setting the Agenda for the 21st Century 185

Introduction to Chapter 12 185

Contributors

James F. Birren, Ph.D., is director of the Institute for Advanced Study and professor of psychology and gerontology at the University of Southern California. Dr. Birren serves on the boards of the Gerontological Society of America, the Western Gerontological Society, the American Psychological Association, and the recently founded Alliance for Aging Research. He is also an advisor to the World Health Organization.

Cyril F. Brickfield, chairman of the Leadership Council of Aging Organizations, was executive director of the American Association of Retired Persons, a 24-million-member organization, for 11 years. He established the first nursing home system for the Veterans Administration, where he served as deputy director.

William E. Brock, Secretary of Labor from 1985 to 1988, served on the Economic Policy Council, the President's Task Force on Regulatory Relief, the President's Advisory Council on Private Sector Initiatives, and other senior governmental councils and committees. Mr. Brock, a former member of the U.S. Senate (R-TN), elected in 1970, served on the Finance Committee, Banking Committee, and Government Operations Committee. He has become a strong advocate for the needs of older workers.

Robert N. Butler, M.D., is Brookdale Professor and Chairman of the Gerald and May Ellen Ritter Department of Geriatrics and Adult Development at the Mount Sinai School of Medicine in New York City, the nation's first medical school department of geriatrics. Dr. Butler was founding director of the National Institute on Aging (1975–1982). In 1976 he won the Pulitzer Prize for his book *Why Survive? Being Old in America*. Dr. Butler is editor-in-chief of the journal *Geriatrics*, chairs programs for the Commonwealth and Brookdale foundations, served on the U.S. Congress Physicians Payment Review Commission, and sits on the boards of many of the country's leading associations.

David R. Carpenter, chairman of the board, president, and chief executive officer of the Transamerica Life Companies in Los Angeles, is the national chairman of the Alliance for Aging Research and a director of the American Council of Life Insurance.

Carl W. Cotman, Ph.D., is professor of psychobiology, neurology, and psychiatry at the University of California, Irvine, specializing in the chemistry of the nervous system. He serves on the National Institute on Aging Task Force and the advisory board of the Alzheimer's Disease and Related Disorders Association.

Hugh Downs currently cohosts ABC's television program "20/20." He is well informed about the problems of the aging, as indicated in his innovative television program "Over Easy." He was one of the initial hosts of the "Today Show," staying with that television program for nine years. Mr. Downs has written six books. One, entitled *Thirty Dirty Lies About Old Age*, debunks myths about aging.

Jean K. Elder, Ph.D., acting assistant secretary, Office of Human Development Services, Department of Health and Human Services, is responsible for administering programs of more than $5 billion, including those involving the elderly, the disabled, and low-income families. An educational psychologist, she has served as commissioner of the Administration on Developmental Disabilities since 1972.

Amitai Etzioni, Ph.D., founder and director of the Center for Policy Research, holds the rank of University Professor at George Washington University, where he teaches sociology. An advisor to the White House in 1979/1980, Etzioni was a guest scholar at the Brookings Institution in 1978/1979. The author of some 14 books, Dr. Etzioni is a consultant to corporations and governmental departments. His views are often expressed in *The Washington Post, The New York Times,* and *Psychology Today.*

Arthur S. Flemming, J.D., is presently co-chairman of the Save Our Security (SOS) Coalition. A former secretary of Health, Education, and Welfare, Dr. Flemming was chairman of the U.S. Commission on Civil Rights from 1974 until 1982. Distinguished for his work in aging, Mr. Flemming was chairman of the 1971 White House Conference on Aging and co-chairman of the 1981 conference, where he led efforts to retain social security benefits.

Douglas A. Fraser is a professor of labor studies at Wayne State University and a fellow and lecturer at the John F. Kennedy School at Harvard University. He was president of the United Auto Workers from 1977 until his retirement in 1983. A skillful negotiator, Fraser had a hand in unifying the UAW and the AFL-CIO and in promoting health and pension benefits for workers.

Betty Friedan's 1963 book, *The Feminine Mystique,* ignited the Women's Movement. Her more recent book, *The Second Stage,* tracks the social evolution of that movement. Now turning her attention to older women, Ms. Friedan, a 1986 fellow at the Andrus Center for Gerontology, writes about the "mystique of aging."

Herbert Gleason, secretary of the Salzburg Seminar, is an attorney with the firm of Mason and Martin in Boston. He serves on several health advisory boards for the city of Boston and was editor of *Productive Aging* and a *Report on Health Care* from the Salzburg Seminar.

John Glenn (D-OH), well known for his many contributions to our national life, is an advocate of basic research on aging and an observer of national and international repercussions of population aging. He became a member of the Senate Special Committee on Aging in 1977 and remained on that committee until the 100th Congress. In 1980 he chaired a hearing entitled "How Old is Old? The Effect of Aging on Learning and Working." In 1985, he chaired a hearing on "The Greying of Nations" at the International Congress of Gerontology.

Louis Harris, noted for his analyses of public opinion, writes a syndicated newspaper column and is a contributor to *Business Week,* as well as a regular political commentator for National Public Radio. His company, Louis Harris and Associates, has conducted more than 5,000 surveys, among them *Myth and Reality of Aging in America,* commissioned by the National Council on Aging in 1974, and, more recently, *Aging in the Eighties: America in Transition,* also for NCOA.

Orrin Hatch, (R-UT), ranking minority member of the U.S. Committee on Labor and Human Resources, has been actively involved in the reauthorization of legislation concerning the Older Americans

Act, both as chairman and conferee. Senator Hatch has sponsored legislation for Medicare reform emphasizing home health care, and has been a strong proponent of protecting funds appropriated to the National Institutes of Health.

Edward M. Kennedy (D-MA) is chairman of the Senate Committee on Labor and Human Resources, which has legislative responsibility for the programs of the Public Health Service. Senator Kennedy's chairmanship involves him in policy making of legislation concerning jobs and trade, access to health services, biomedical research, preventive medicine, catastrophic health insurance, and AIDS. A senator for 25 years, Mr. Kennedy authored the Family Practice of Medicine Act, the Rehabilitation Act (the nation's first civil rights bill for disabled persons) and the law that helped establish the first ethics commission for protection of human subjects in biomedical research.

Kenzo Kiikuni, managing director of the Sasakawa Memorial Health Foundation, is also a professor at the Institute of Medicine at the University of Tsukuba. Mr. Kiikuni is on the board of the Japanese Society on Hospital Administration and is science councilor for the Japan Medical Education Foundation.

Takao Komine is director of research for Japan's Fair Trade Commission. Prior to joining the commission, he was a staff economist for the Economic Planning Agency, worked on the report *Japan in the Year 2000* and authored several books on economic matters.

F. Peter Libassi is senior vice president of the Travelers Companies. He was general counsel for the U.S. Department of Health, Education, and Welfare from 1977 to 1979. Prior to joining the staff of Travelers, Mr. Libassi was a partner in Verner, Liipfert, Bernhard, McPherson, & Hand, where he tracked legislative issues.

Daisaku Maeda, director of the Department of Sociology at the Tokyo Metropolitan Institute of Gerontology, is a member of the National Advisory Council on Social Welfare and the Advisory Council on Statistical Investigation for the Minister of Health and Welfare in Japan. He serves on the Advisory Panel on Health of Elderly Persons for the United Nation's World Health Organization. Widely published in both Japan and the United States, Dr. Maeda also serves on the editorial boards of journals on geriatrics and gerontology published around the world.

Spark Matsunaga (D-HI), in his second term as senator, is known internationally for his role in the creation and development of the Pacific International Center for High Technology Research. Senator Matsunaga serves on the Finance, Labor and Human Resources, and the Veterans Affairs committees. As chairman of the Labor Committee's Subcommittee on Aging, he advocated the reauthorization of the Older Americans Act.

John Melcher (D-MT) was chairman of the U.S. Senate's Special Committee on Aging and a member of the Joint Economic Committee of Congress. He sponsored legislation to address the financial catastrophes of illness, and fought proposals that would have increased out-of-pocket health care costs for the elderly and the disabled.

Thomas W. Moloney, senior vice president of the Commonwealth Fund, is responsible for all health-related programs for the foundation. He is chairman of the board of Grantmakers in Health and serves on numerous other boards. A fellow of the American Association for the Advancement of Science, he sits on the Board of Visitors of the University of California, Davis, School of Medicine.

Shigenobu Nakamura, Ph.D., is associate professor of the Department of Neurology at Kyoto University in Japan. From 1968 to 1980, he was a research associate in the Department of Geriatric Medicine at Kyoto University.

Tadashi Nakamura, assistant minister for International Labor Affairs in Japan, entered the Ministry of Labor in 1958. He is chairman of the Manpower and Social Affairs Committee of the Organization of Economic Cooperation and Development.

Osamu Nishio, who developed mechatronics—the combination of mechanical and electronic engineering—as well as innovative personnel practices for Okuma Machinery, was named Okuma's New York president in 1985. He has since established a manufacturing plant in North Carolina.

Claude Pepper, (D-FL), recently deceased, was noted for his dedication, perseverance, and imagination that led to the passage of the amendments to the Age Discrimination and Employment Act of 1967, virtually bringing an end to mandatory retirement. His long service in Congress, dating from the 1930s until his death in 1989, included terms as a senator as well as representative and established him as a conscientious, knowledgeable, and productive member of Congress. As chairman of the House Rules Committee, he was in a pivotal position to advance legislation in health and social welfare for Americans of all ages. At the time of his death, he was chairman of the Congressional Bipartisan Commission on Comprehensive Care.

Marion A. Perlmutter, Professor of Psychology at the University of Michigan, is also Associate Director of the university's Institute of Gerontology and a research scientist at its Center for Human Growth and Development. She serves on the executive boards of the Gerontological Society of America, the American Psychological Association, the Society for Research in Child Development, and the International Society for the Study of Behavioral Development. She is an advisor to the National Institute of Aging and an associate editor for the Journal of Developmental Psychology and Comprehensive Gerontology.

Esther Peterson, an early activist in the American labor movement, has had a long and distinguished career in labor, women's issues, and consumer affairs, serving three U.S. presidents. She has been director of the Women's Bureau in the Labor Department and has served on the Commission on the Status of Women and the Consumer Affairs Council.

Larry Pressler (R-SD) is a member of the Senate Special Committee on Aging, where he is a leading proponent of Alzheimer's disease research. Senator Pressler is also an active member of the Foreign Relations Committee's Near Eastern and South Asian Affairs Subcommittee.

Ralph Regula (D-OH) is a ranking member of the House Select Committee on Aging's Subcommittee on Health and Long-Term Care. He has introduced bills on catastrophic expense protection and long-term care. He has been an active proponent of Medicare reform and, together with Representative Claude Pepper, introduced legislation to establish Alzheimer's disease treatment centers.

John W. Rowe, M.D., is president and chief executive officer of the Mount Sinai Medical Center in New York City. Formerly he was the director of the Division of Aging at Harvard Medical School and a professor of medicine and chief of the gerontology division at Beth Israel Hospital in Boston. Long active in policy aspects of geriatric medicine, Dr. Rowe's special interest is the normal physiology of aging.

Edward Roybal (D-CA), chairman of the House Select Committee on Aging, has served on the Committee since 1975. Over the past two decades, he has championed adequate health care, housing, and social services for the elderly. He has opposed mandatory retirement practices, offered legislation to protect workers' pensions, and sought to maintain federal support for programs for all older Americans.

Patricia Saiki (R-HI), a third-generation Japanese-American, is the first Republican Asian-American woman to serve in Congress. During her 13 years in the Hawaii legislature before coming to Washington, she helped pioneer health, education, and women's rights legislation. Her strong interest in these areas continues in the U.S. Congress, in addition to her work on the House Select Committee on Aging.

James Sasser (D-TN) has sponsored a number of bills that address the issues of the aging population. He introduced legislation focused upon restructuring Medicare and setting up 10 centers of excellence in geriatric research and training, which would help train the great numbers of geriatric practitioners and health care workers this country will need by the end of this century.

Richard Scammon has been director of the Elections Research Center since 1955. Mr. Scammon served as a member of several U.S. commissions sent abroad to monitor local elections, including the 1967 President's commission to observe elections in Vietnam and the 1982 delegation to observe elections in El Salvador. Mr. Scammon is editor of the *America Votes* series, Volumes 1 to 17, spanning the period from 1956 to 1987.

Claudine Schneider (R-RI) is widely recognized as a leader on behalf of older Americans. She is an active member of the House Select Committee on Aging and the House Science and Technology Committee. Before her election to Congress in 1980, Representative Schneider was active in energy and environmental issues, as well as health affairs.

Edward L. Schneider, M.D., is Dean of the University of Southern California's Ethel Percy Andrus Gerontology Center. A former deputy director of the National Institute on Aging, Dr. Schneider taught at Johns Hopkins and other universities. Among the many publications he has edited is the *Handbook of the Biology of Aging.* Dr. Schneider serves on the editorial boards of five publications in gerontology and geriatrics.

Daniel J. Schulder, senior public policy associate for the National Council on the Aging, worked on the staff of the 1981 White House

Conference on Aging and was the former director of the aging program for the Office of Equal Opportunity.

Joan Smith-Sonneborn, Ph.D., professor of the Department of Zoology and Physiology at the University of Wyoming, is active in the Gerontological Society of America. She has served on its key committees and is now a member of the Executive Council. She chaired the Biology of Aging committee for the Gordon Conference.

Alvar Svanborg, M.D., Ph.D., is chief of the Section of Geriatric Medicine at the University of Illinois in Chicago. He was Sweden's delegate to the United Nations World Assembly on Aging in 1982 and was an advisor to the U.S. Government in 1985 on the "Greying of Nations II." He formerly was the chairman of geriatric and long-term care medicine at Sweden's University of Gothenburg and is known internationally for his work on the physiological and psychological aspects of aging.

Toru Tsumita, M.D., director of the Tokyo Metropolitan Institute of Gerontology, is also professor emeritus of the University of Tokyo, where he taught from 1960 until his retirement in 1985.

Sumio Yoshida, M.D., has been president of the Well Aging Association of Japan since 1981. A former government official, Dr. Yoshida is on the Board of the Japan Gerontology Society and the Japan World Health Organization Association.

Foreword

I was born on May 4, 1899; thus I will become 88 this year. I'm blessed with good health, I do not need glasses to read, and I work 365 days a year because I believe that I will have plenty of holidays when I get to the other world.

My motto is "The world is one big family." I try to share my good health with all the people in this world who still do not have equal access to the outcomes of the scientific technology that we have developed. I hope to bring happiness, health, and longevity to all people by making this space of ours a little cleaner, more comfortable, and more peaceful place to live. I believe that everyone on this earth should contribute his or her share toward the health and happiness of mankind. If you have energy, you will fight. If you have creativity, you will fight. If you have resources, you will fight. I may be enjoying excellent health, but I should not be enjoying it by myself; it should be shared with many people on this earth. Thus I created the Sasakawa Memorial Health Foundation on my 75th birthday in the hope of promoting international cooperation to tackle various health problems in this world.

Certainly the problem of aging is one of the most difficult problems of this age of rapid changes. Although nothing seems to be certain, one thing for sure is that we all age, and mankind has yet to find an adequate solution to the problem of staying productive in old age. However, I'm confident that if we unite our energy, creativity, and resources, we'll most surely find a way to overcome this difficult problem. Money is useless unless it is put to good use. We were all born naked and we will die with nothing to carry over to another world. Money must be effectively used for the welfare of the people of this world.

Although I am now physically 88 years old, I have decided to discard 60 years and become a youthful 28. I believe any age beyond 60 is like a thief trying to steal one's life, so I neither welcome nor celebrate its arrival. I have been telling people to plant a tree on their birthday instead of celebrating with a birthday cake. Trees not only clean our air but please our eyes.

I shall continue to serve mankind to the best of my ability. I also pray for the prosperity of all the people in all the countries of the world: for their health, happiness, and longevity.

RYOICHI SASAKAWA
Chairman,
Japan Shipbuilding
Industry Foundation

Preface

Industrial societies throughout the world are beginning to recognize that they are facing the challenge of productive aging—a task unique in human history, because this is the first time industrialized countries have such large elderly populations. For millions of elderly citizens, life span is no longer three-score years and ten, but more like four-score years and seven. This unique situation is one that we applaud. All of us, if we are fortunate, will one day be old. But it also creates unprecedented challenges that must be met if the additional years of life are to be a gift and not a crisis.

One of our most serious challenges is to maintain physical health and mental vigor as we age. We reject the stereotype of old age as years of senility and decline. The fictional Mr. Dooley once said: "Old fellows like you and me cluck about the advantages of age. We have wisdom, but we'd rather have hair; we have experience, but we'd trade it all for hope and teeth." Aldous Huxley put it even more pessimistically: "The aging man of the 20th century lives not in the public world of atomic physics and conflicting ideologies, of welfare states and supersonic speed, but in his strictly private universe of physical weakness and mental decay." If Mr. Dooley and Mr. Huxley were here today, they would probably be eating their words, because in the late 1980s they are far from true.

We know from the many exceptional older people who live among us that they remain vigorous and productive in mind and body. Former President Reagan himself provided ample proof that advancing years do not mean declining abilities and responsibilities.

But too many senior citizens are not blessed with happy and productive retirement years. For some, this loss can be traced to specific illnesses like stroke, arthritis, or Alzheimer's disease. In others the reasons for decline are more difficult to understand. To me, one of the highest priorities of health research should be to identify and deal with the organic causes that rob our senior citizens of their golden years. Indeed, prevention or cure for Alzheimer's disease alone could empty a large part of the nation's nursing homes.

Not only physical illness denies senior citizens the opportunity for productive old age. There is also the all-too-frequent failure of society to provide reasonable social and economic supports for activities that not only prolong life but make life worth living. In fact, the most immediate challenge is to assure the availability of essential health care services. In the United States, despite the enactment of Medicare and Medicaid, far too many senior citizens are deprived of their life savings. They lose all hope for comfortable and secure retirement because of the unfair financial burden of serious illness.

Even apart from the devastating cost of nursing home care each year, almost a quarter of all senior citizens paying for health care have expenses that are catastrophic by any realistic standard. The primary sources of these catastrophic costs are Medicare's high co-payments, high deductibles, and essential services it does not cover at all. Cost of nursing home care is potentially the most devastating of all. Here Medicare benefits are minimal. Medicaid is available only after the patient is impoverished, and impoverishment often comes soon after the first bill. Almost two-thirds of all single senior citizens would be impoverished by a nursing home stay of just three months. Of those who are married, one-third would be impoverished in the same short time, and more than half would be impoverished within a year. This spectre of destitution as the result of serious illness and the need for long-term care confronts more and more elderly Americans. Five percent of those over 65 are already residents of nursing homes, and one-quarter more will spend a portion of their lives in one.

This state of affairs is unacceptable. It is time for Congress to restore the promise of Medicaid and make it once again the symbol of hope for the low-income elderly who are ill, and not the sword of Damocles threatening poverty for the remainder of their years. Other countries do a better job of protecting their senior citizens against the high cost of uninsured illness. It is time for the United States to join the ranks of those who recognize that health care for the elderly is not just a privilege for the wealthy few, but a basic human right for all.

The final challenge that our society confronts in this area is an economic one. The portion of senior citizens in our total population is rising. Current work and retirement patterns are likely to result in increased burdens on the young to provide for their support. Unless we have the wisdom to deal in advance with these changing demographic facts, support for social insurance programs will inevitably decline.

To ward off such trends, we must do whatever we can to ensure that research in aging continues to be supported. Policies, programs, and research that contribute to healthier and more productive aging benefit not just the current generation of elderly, but also the children and workers of today who will be the senior citizens of tomorrow.

EDWARD M. KENNEDY
Senator of Massachusetts

Preface

Within the next 50 years, the segment of the population aged 65 and older will more than double, and the number of people 75 years and older will more than triple. We are undergoing a profound demographic transformation as the result of major increases in life expectancy in combination with the end of the baby boom. Along with these developments come certain responsibilities. We must make every effort to ensure that older Americans are not just cared for, but are also leading happy and productive lives. They are a treasure of skill and experience, and, to remain competitive in international trade, America cannot afford to disregard them.

We have to face the fact that because this country is growing older, some changes must occur in our attitudes and our programs. We know that our country will benefit greatly from increased numbers of healthy, long-lived citizens. At the same time, it could suffer enormous losses if its older population is ill, functionally dependent, and socially inactive.

In 1960, Japan had about 8.5 working people for every one retired. This figure has dropped to 6.1, and by the year 2000 it will be 3.9. Consequently, productivity must rise just to maintain the standard of living. The United States is in a similar state of evolution. Today, the United States is the most productive country in the history of the world. But can we maintain our leadership role with an increased quality of life? The economy is strong. We have the highest percentage ever of people working, the lowest inflation rate in over 20 years, and the highest rate of improvement in our manufacturing product since 1950. Interest rates are 75% lower than they were 7 years ago. The only jobs that have decreased in the last 5 years are those in the minimum-wage category. Jobs paying over $10 an hour have increased by over 50%, while minimum-wage jobs have decreased by 25%. That is where we are. But where are we going to be in the year 2000?

We have a good idea of what the workplace of the nation will look like in the year 2000, what the strains on the average worker will be, and what needs to be done for this nation to stay competitive. Our work force has been growing at about 3% a year over the last few decades, but the growth will slow to 1%. The work force will age rapidly from an average age of 35 years to 39 years. The demographic composition of the new entrants will change; 80% will comprise women, minorities, and immigrants. These three groups have been traditionally disadvantaged and will, in particular, require improved skill development programs. In addition, since low-paying and low-skill jobs are rapidly disappearing, we will soon have a major problem because 30% of students entering high school do not finish and 40% of those who do cannot read at the ninth-grade level. Our public school system is not well tended or supported, and we have to change that fast. We have 23 million functional illiterates in the United States who cannot read at the fourth-grade level and cannot hold jobs.

We have two choices: We either take these inadequately skilled people and give them a skill quickly, or use those who have skills more effectively and for longer periods of time. We will probably have to do both to maintain our economic growth. If we continue with what we are doing now, within the next two or three years we will simply run out of people with adequate skills to hold the 200,000 jobs created each month. Yet, in the face of all this, we are continuing to talk about early retirement and stopping training for any person older than 50. We are going to pay if we do not change this soon.

With competitiveness the problem is not where we are so much as where we are headed in relationship to what other countries are doing. The problem is a human question of what we are doing, not just for our young people or our adults, but for our older adult workers and citizens. As we move from an industrial society to the bio-tech age, there is a lot of turmoil in the marketplace. The average graduate today will hold four to six jobs in his or her lifetime, probably in two or three careers. Most are not doing this by choice but, rather, because jobs are changing right underneath their feet. What happens then to their pensions? We run the very serious long-term risk that those workers will end up without an adequate pension because they have been forced to change jobs but were unable to take their pension investments with them. We have to quickly address the need for portability in the pension system. It is not simple; it is going to require a good deal of intellectual energy and, perhaps, capital. Pension plans have seen phenomenal growth, but employees now need to be able to take their pensions with them.

We all have a role to play in the development of this productive society. We should establish this as a new ethic: Everybody has the right to work as long as she or he wants to and can. This would aid productivity and help fill the need for skills. Also, it is good for individuals to continue to feel productive and needed. We are creating more jobs than we have entrants for. There is a hunger for skills and this, in turn, is creating an urgency for management to respond by trying to develop new ways to maintain those skills in the marketplace. We need to encourage that. We need also to encourage the kind of work that keeps people healthy and productive in advancing years.

We are making incredible progress as a society, as a people, as a community of the world, and in giving people not only longer lives but also healthier and more productive ones. This is important to the productivity of this country. We will continue our research and our efforts in that sense, but it is also important that we understand that everybody—adult, senior citizen, or child— needs, more than anything else, to feel needed, to be productive, and to have a sense of self-worth. By encouraging, supporting, nurturing, and sustaining that, we not only contribute to them, but we also contribute immeasurably to our own well-being.

WILLIAM E. BROCK
U.S. Secretary of Labor 1985–1988

Acknowledgments

The "Promise of Productive Aging" symposium was sponsored by the Japan Shipbuilding Industry Foundation, hosted by the Alliance for Aging Research, and conducted by the Center for Productive Aging of the Gerald and May Ellen Ritter Department of Geriatrics and Adult Development at the Mount Sinai School of Medicine in New York City. (For further information about the Japan Shipbuilding Industry Foundation, the Alliance for Aging Research, and the Gerald and May Ellen Ritter Department of Geriatrics and Adult Development, see Appendix A.)

We would like to thank the following supporting organizations: American Association for International Aging; American Medical Association; The Brookdale Foundation; Economic Planning Agency—Japanese Government; Embassy of Japan; Japan American Society of Washington; Japan External Trade Organization; Japan Productivity Center—U.S. Office; Japanese-American Citizens League National Committee on Aging and Retirement; National Institute on Aging; Population Resources Center; Tokyo Metropolitan Institute on Gerontology; United Nations World Health Organization; U.S. Congressional Clearinghouse on the Future; U.S. House Select Committee on Aging; U.S. Senate Special Committee on Aging; and Well-Aging Association of Japan.

We are also grateful to the following organizations whose

generosity and support were essential to the success of the symposium: Allied-Signal, Inc.; American Association of Retired Persons; Florida Power & Light Company; MetPath, Inc., A Corning Laboratory Science Company; The Monsanto Company; Evelyn Stefansson Nef; Paul F. Glenn Foundation for Medical Research; SmithKline Beckman Corporation; and The Upjohn Company.

Finally, we are especially appreciative of the Brookdale Foundations generosity in providing support for the preparation of this book.

R.N.B.
M.R.O.
M.S.

Introduction

In less than a century, both Japan and the United States have gained a spectacular 25 years in average life expectancy at birth. This gain has come about not only for medical reasons but because of broad social progress. It reflects advances in the control of infectious diseases, in sanitation, nutrition, and maternal and child health, and in other factors that have improved our standards of living. About 20% of the gain in overall life expectancy is due to the reduction of mortality rates in the later years of life.

An aging population will be the dominant fact of life for American and Japanese societies well into the 21st century. By the year 2025, over 20% of both the Japanese and American populations will be 65 and older. Both nations will continue to experience dramatic increases in the absolute number of elderly people and the proportion of elderly relative to younger members of society.

Some observers have feared that, with this new longevity and population aging, societies will have great difficulties in dealing with income maintenance, claims upon services for health care, and other issues associated with aging. History teaches us, however, that productivity grows in proportion to longevity. Societies in which illness, disability, and infectious disease truncate longevity cannot hope to be as productive as societies that are longer living.

The purpose of the symposium "The Promise of Productive Aging," which took place in Washington, DC, on April 28–29, 1987, and whose proceedings are recorded in this book, was to discuss these concerns and provide a sound and positive understanding of human aging. The symposium had several sources. In 1982 at the Salzburg Seminar, the participants focused on the concept of *productive aging:* the notion that we can, and must, express and facilitate our personal and social productivity as we grow older.[1] This means building programs that assist physically frail and dependent elderly people to make the most of their opportunities. But we must also focus upon that even larger, growing population of older people who are robust and intellectually active, and who possess a great reservoir of wisdom, knowledge, and experience.

Another source was the book *Japan in the Year 2000,* a thoughtful and valuable analysis of 21st-century Japan, created by the Japan Economic Planning Agency.[2] Japanese officials have clearly indicated that population aging is one of three key factors in Japan's development as it enters the next century.

It is important to note here that Japan and the United States share much in common. We are basically good and important friends. We both have worked toward mobilizing the continuing productivity of our people by elevating the retirement age. We both have great institutes of gerontology: the Tokyo Metropolitan Institute of Gerontology and the National Institute on Aging. These two institutions have an agreement to share scholars and scientific information and participate in a variety of collaborations.

A third source was the book *Modern Biological Theories of Aging,*[3] in which leading scientists summarize the many complex biological theories of aging. Some of these scientists participated in the "Promise of Productive Aging" symposium and

[1] Butler, R. N., & Gleason, H. P. (Ed.) (1985). *Productive aging. Enhancing vitality in later life.* New York: Springer.
[2] Long-Term Outlook Committee, Economic Council, Economic Planning Agency. (1983). *Japan in the year 2000.* Tokyo: The Japan Times, Ltd.
[3] Warner, H. R., Butler, R. N., Sprott, R. L., & Schneider, E. L. (Eds.). (1987). Modern biological theories of aging. New York: Raven Press.

presented current scientific facts about aging upon which the
principles of productive aging are built. Because of the relevance of these facts to any discussion about productive aging,
we saw fit to publish these contributors' papers in full in Parts I
and II of this book. (An exception is Joan Smith-Sonneborn's
chapter, which, because of its length, is summarized in Part I.)

The science of gerontology is not only the study of aging, that
is, the processes operating throughout our lifetimes that increase our vulnerability to disability and disease, but also the
study of longevity. Furthermore, gerontology studies not only
the quantity of life in old age but also its quality. When the
National Institute on Aging was created, its purpose was
clearly stated: "To expand the prime middle years of life." No
one wishes to extend the length of life if it is not going to be
vital, satisfying, and productive. The study of aging is multidimensional and interdisciplinary. The more the disciplines of
science, clinical practice, socioeconomic analysis, the humani-
ties, and other fields interact with one another, the more we
will benefit from their collaboration. This is why the "Promise
of Productive Aging" symposium brought together such diverse
individuals from such diverse perspectives. Frankly, it is a hazardous thing to do. When one brings together scientists, scholars, intellectuals, policymakers, and politicians, one runs the
risk of generating confusion through conflicting points of view
in differing languages.

But since we wanted to present a broad picture of productive
aging, we involved an unusual mixture of people who have
something to contribute to the puzzle. If we are going to speak
sensibly about human productivity, we have to understand how
and in what ways we change—cognitively and physiologically.
We have to discuss the possibilities for medical intervention in
the processes of aging. We have to examine the potentials for an
extended worklife and the cultural, social, economic, and political implications of rapidly aging societies. These were the goals
for the symposium, which proved to be a forum for many stimulating discussions. We have tried to reproduce these here as
faithfully as possible in as authentic and as lively a format as we
could find.

As we grow older, we will be better off if we have a continuing, positive, and substantial role to play in our family, community, and nation. It is to society's advantage that we continue to contribute to it, rather than only make claims upon it. Both society and individuals are served by efforts to promote productive aging.

ROBERT N. BUTLER, M.D.
Brookdale Professor and Chairman,
Gerald and May Ellen Ritter Department of
Geriatrics and Adult Development
Mount Sinai School of Medicine

Human Aging and Intervention

I

Note on the Support of Aging Research

The Alliance for Aging Research is a new partnership of science, government, and the private sector in the United States. Its formation marks the coming of age of the political power behind the growing popular support for aging research. We seek to advance gerontology and preventive geriatrics by bringing together, as we are here, leading scientists, executives, foundation leaders, and members of Congress to study the issues and get things done. We wish to advance aging research as a national priority.

The steep costs of health care and long-term care could overwhelm public and private resources as the U.S. baby boomers mature over the next 25 years. By the year 2000, the elderly will be incurring one-half of all U.S. health expenses. By 2040, Alzheimer's disease and other dementias will affect five times as many victims as there are today. By mid-century, four times as many people will need long-term care. That is, unless science can intervene. We have a clear choice: Suffer the consequences of an ill, dependent, older population, or benefit from a more healthy, productive, and longer-living one. That's the promise of aging research—health and vitality in all stages of life. The key question is: Are we prepared to invest in aging research today so that we can earn dividends tomorrow?

Leading scientists in gerontology believe that large-scale, lifetime health and vigor are definitely attainable in the foreseeable future. Research can be the fulcrum, transforming more and

3

more of our elderly into a rich resource. The obvious must be said: We cannot afford *not* to treat older Americans as a productive resource. If we don't begin to change our ways now, we will not be able to solve the socioeconomic problems that lie before us. We're past the beginning steps of research. Next, we can look forward to disease intervention, treatment, rehabilitation, and even some intervention in the aging processes. We're moving toward a few testable theories of human aging, a great opportunity for future learning.

The benefits of aging research for the United States, Japan, and the entire world are there for us to reap, but we must work together. We need government's leadership and support. We cannot afford to let the momentum slow; we cannot afford to let the funding slip for research in neurology, immunology, oncology, cardiology, arthritis, mental illness, hearing, and vision. We cannot afford to skimp on our support for the National Institute on Aging (NIA).

The NIA research outlays are still quite small in comparison with health costs. The fiscal 1987 NIA budget, $177 million, was already small. Yet, the Administration recommended a decrease of $11 million for 1988. The budget for NIA's Alzheimer's Disease Program is approximately $50 million, but the yearly cost of this disease is $40 billion.

Congress is now working on next year's budget. Before the year is over, Congress and the Administration will have determined what should be the proper level of support for the NIA and many other units of government that carry out research relating to aging. The Alliance for Aging Research hopes to make a contribution to those negotiations. We hope to work with both the legislative and executive branches of government to raise the priority of aging research not only this year, but for years to come.

Time does not stand still. The demographic imperative is too urgent now for *us* to stand still.

DAVID R. CARPENTER
Chairman of the Board,
President, and Chief Executive Officer
Transamerica Life Companies

Introduction to Part I

Three scientists present a current review and discuss the prospects for scientific research into processes of aging. Their facts and views provide policymakers with a strong basis for hope: Not only does science indicate that more years can be added to average human life, but the odds of making the added years healthy rather than sick can be raised. This expectation is central to the conference objective of linking policy and science for the purpose of facilitating productive aging. Policymakers and the public could see research as having the potential to resolve conflicts over the distribution of resources among old and young, well and sick, and health care and other domains of consumption.

Dr. Joan Smith-Sonneborn provides policymakers and other lay people with a broad-ranging review of scientific research bearing on normal aging and age-related disease. Progress in many disciplines of science has benefited investigators studying processes of aging. For example, simple gene interventions have complex physiological effects. Investigators in aging may follow these effects over the years as animals age.

Dr. Toru Tsumita provides us with a life-cycle view of processes of aging. What are the earliest precursors of later life manifestations of normal aging and age-related diseases? The possibility of intervention in harmful processes of aging at a time when they may be more readily counteracted intrigues Dr. Tsumita. Based on classifications of processes, he offers the concept of a multilevel approach to finding possible interventions.

Should we intervene in processes of aging? Dr. Edward Schneider provides policymakers with an affirmative answer, grounded in achievements in the control of coronary artery disease. Similar achievements, he believes, will emerge from improved understanding of Alzheimer's disease, the human immune system, and metabolic anomalies.

All three scientists leave the impression that research into processes of aging is a fertile area, with harvests to come all the more surely and rapidly if sound investment in research is practiced. What may be the most provocative statement and challenge from the scientists was articulated by Dr. Smith-Sonneborn: The age at which all of us age is determined by our societies, as are decisions to invest in science, education, and service. "We are in a position to intervene in the tragic waste of our mind and body with age," she says, adding: "Accept the challenge."

How We Age

1

Joan Smith-Sonneborn

The image of how we age is derived from examining: (1) theories of aging, (2) correlates of species specific life span determinants, (3) genetic diseases with early onset of aspects of aging, and (4) environmentally induced aging symptoms.

No single theory of aging captures all aspects of either causes or symptoms of aging; rather, different theories provide insight into their interactive role in changes with age. Aging is a programmed process whose composition is set during formation of the embryo when species-specific levels of pro-aging and pro-longevity factors are determined. Master gene complexes may control suites of genes that have an impact on longevity. Such gene suites may include those that regulate deoxyribonucleic acid (DNA) repair, scavengers of free radicals, immune histocompatibility, metabolic rate factors, and numbers of critical cell types in the central nervous system (CNS).

Once assembled, the individual molecules, cells, and organs, like members of a symphony, interact as a unit. The CNS acts as the conductor, sending timed signals to target organs which respond with their appropriate contribution. The reciprocal interactions regulate the balance of excitatory and inhibitory responses. During aging, the interactions between the command and target tissues change.

MOLECULAR CHANGES

Alteration of structural molecules induced by both nonenzymatic and enzymatic changes occur with aging. Such changes, for example, can contribute to rigidity of arteries, lenses, and membranes of the ear or lungs, respectively impacting on circulation, sight, hearing, and breathing. Since the same molecules can function in different ways and in different systems, one defect can cascade into multiple pathways of functional losses. DNA repair genes, for example, not only repair DNA; certain sequences in the repair complex may overlap with DNA replication and recombination (both in the germ and somatic cells), affecting movement of jumping genes and antibody formation.

DNA damage can contribute to inappropriate gene expression associated with increased risk of cancer, immune disorders, and senility. Free-radical-induced molecular changes theoretically can contribute to emphysema, atherosclerosis, cancer, osteoarthritis, cirrhosis, and diabetes.

CELLULAR CHANGES

Programmed cell aging is imposed on omnipotent cells. Certain cells retain the ability to access all menus, or at least different menus. Regeneration is possible for selected organs in man, even into advanced age. Thus, cell aging is not an inevitable quality of life. Loss of the ability to divide is associated with the presence of antidivision messages and proteins.

Reduced division potential of cells lining the arterial wall, for example, can lead to an inability to keep pace with induced damage. Deposits of excess cholesterol complexes can then accumulate in the exposed inner layer, contributing to atherosclerotic lesions and associated disorders.

Cells in the CNS have different signal receivers. Selective loss of either excitatory or inhibitory receptors can lead to specific patterns of functional losses. Corticosteroid excess, for example, induced by age, stress, genetic predisposition, or hormonal triggers, can destroy the hippocampal region of the brain, causing associated functional losses in memory and the immune system.

Threshold damage can accumulate in days or years before the functional defect is expressed.

Selective loss of certain dopamine receptors in the substantia nigra region of the brain can contribute to movement disorders, stooped posture, and shuffle-gait walking. In animal models, drugs that allow for the restoration of receptors or involve transplants of tissue to damaged brain regions can at least partially restore youthful motor function.

In metabolic pathways, differences in proteins that transport or receptors that accept blood cholesterol complexes can lead to differences in cholesterol clearance, in drug and diet response, and in risk of coronary heart disease. One man's cure is another man's poison.

Drugs that test negative in the overall population may affect a 100% cure in those with a specific genetic defect. Variation in genetics has been estimated to account for 50% of the risk for coronary heart disease and may well contribute substantially to the estimated 30,000 deaths per year due to adverse drug reactions, costing between $1 billion to $3 billion for care.

ORGAN CHANGES

Reciprocal interactions between organs and the brain can induce organ deterioration, for example, in the female reproductive system. Hormone excesses and deficits have their own patterns of undesirable fallouts. Many old organs are capable of quality response, but often either a delayed reaction time or an increased stimulation threshold becomes necessary for response. Alteration of inappropriate hormone production has already been effective for partial restoration of a youthful response in insulin level control.

THE ENVIRONMENT

Physical and chemical agents can damage DNA, adding to the age-induced increased vulnerability to damage. The additive effects of age and environmental insults can accelerate early onset

of functional losses. Any agents, like the contaminants of the
designer drug heroin, viral infections, pollution, and food poi-
sons can contribute to threshold levels of neuronal loss with a
characteristic spectrum of functional losses, producing Parkinson's disease. Impairments can vary from mild to severe, depending on the extent of the damage.

THE "HOW" OF AGING

We age, it seems, as individuals, since all of us do not show the
same patterns of age-related defects, with a species-specific life-
time limit. Instead, we age at a rate and pattern specified by our
genetic makeup interacting with our diet and environment.

We are in a biological revolution.

In medical genetics, it is now possible to proceed from a single gene change to its complex physiological effect, rather than
proceeding from the complex effects back on the torturous path
to the gene of origin. Gene typing, like blood typing, is already
possible for some with coronary heart risk; a cloned gene probe
is available for families with Alzheimer's disease relatives to determine if risk can be predicted in those yet without symptoms.
Better matches of defect and appropriate therapy may be possible if we act now.

Analysis, which before took years, can now be accomplished
in days. Explosive advances are occurring frequently. The Febru-
ary 20, 1987, issue of *Science* contains eight articles relevant to
aging and aging diseases (Alzheimer's, osteoporosis, immune
recognition pathologies, and arthritis disorders).

Advances in the technology of gene cloning and protein and
gene sequencing and in computer data banks, radioimmuno-
assays, monoclonal antibodies, and shuttle vectors, for example,
coupled with a better appreciation of the basic mechanisms of
aging and disease, allow us to think what only 10 years ago was
unthinkable: to alter the path of aging. We have reached the
feasibility threshold.

For every dollar that is spent on research, about $1,000 is
spent for care of the chronically-ill aged. Underfunding of

research in the biology of aging is no longer justified, for there is real hope for significant intervention in the aging process and its diseases. Fund raising and dispersal strategies are needed now!

I recommend a major analysis of the human genome to locate those regions correlated with age-related pathologies. Family history could help identify where deficits may occur, and a match can be made between genetic defect and response to therapy. Then, if the $70 billion (at minimum) spent for care of Alzheimer's patients, osteoporosis patients, and those with adverse drug reactions alone were also spent for research, we could reduce human suffering and future medical care costs immensely.

Since many age-related changes involve known chemical imbalances, manipulative therapy to restore balance is now a real possibility. Gene therapy or antisense messages may offer intervention correction of pathway disorders.

We will age at a rate that society deems acceptable. We are in the position to intervene in the tragic waste of our minds and bodies with age. Accept the challenge.

Interventions in Aging

2

Edward L. Schneider

I would like to put interventions into the context of gerontology and then present a few examples of present and proposed biological, behavioral, and social interventions for both normal aging processes and the diseases and disorders of aging.

During this century, there has been a profound change in the composition of our population (Guralnik & Schneider, 1987). For the first time in the history of this planet, enormous numbers of individuals are entering the seventh, eighth, ninth, and even the tenth decades of life. However, the additional years of life expectancy may not be entirely comprised of healthy years. In fact, a comprehensive study of health status in Canada over a 27-year period from 1951 to 1978 suggested that most of the years of life expectancy that were added in that time period were years of disability, as measured by limitations in daily activities (Wilkins & Adams, 1983). However, further studies are needed to confirm these findings.

As millions of older Americans enter the decades of susceptibility to the diseases of aging, we will have enormous numbers of disabled (Schneider & Guralnik, 1987) requiring long-term health care. Realizing the fiscal implications of this growth of an older disabled population, policymakers and others are discussing several approaches to reduce the costs of health care. These include reducing reimbursement to health care providers, rationing health care, or providing insurance coverage for long-term care. There is another approach that I believe will be much more effective: a national program dedicated to lengthening the healthy years of life through biomedical, behavioral, and social research.

Aging research is a relatively new area. The National Institute on Aging (NIA) was created in 1974, and significant support for aging research has occurred only in the last ten years. Therefore, it is not surprising that our knowledge of the mechanisms of aging and of age-dependent diseases is still relatively small. Nevertheless, we have developed some interventions that affect age-dependent diseases, and we have the prospect of other interventions that affect other age-dependent disorders, as well as aging processes.

IS AGING UNALTERABLE?

The public certainly believes that certain aging processes can be altered. This is reflected in the multibillion-dollar sales of products promoted to retard, reverse, or arrest aging processes. Unfortunately, these claims are based more on the avarice of the sellers of these products than on any scientific data.

I would like to make the case that certain aging processes are alterable. However, I believe that it is naive to suggest that we will ever find a single "magic bullet" that will cure all aging processes. Our increasing knowledge in gerontology indicates that aging is the sum total of events occurring at the molecular, organelle, cellular, and organ levels. Cancer research is demonstrating that there are multiple mechanisms underlying cancer, and I predict that aging will be found to be even more complex than cancer. I believe that we will be able to develop successful interventions oriented toward specific aging processes, but will not be able to confer immortality with a pill.

SHOULD WE INTERVENE IN
THE AGING PROCESS?

This is a complex issue. A full text could be devoted to discussions of the merits of intervening in aging processes. Literature provides many examples of the negative aspects of arresting aging. Certainly, adding years to life rather than life to years would be a tragedy. But that is exactly what has happened in the last decades without any organized attempt to increase longevity. Aging research could reverse this trend. Through our understanding of aging and age-dependent diseases, we have the potential of extending the healthy years of life and compressing diseases and disability into a few short years. This would certainly be a meritorious goal.

INTERVENTIONS IN AGE-DEPENDENT
DISEASES AND DISORDERS

In the last three decades, we have made remarkable progress in reducing deaths from the leading age-dependent killer: coronary artery disease. While many different groups might claim credit for this accomplishment, it is clear that cardiovascular research played a major role in the conquest of this number-one cause of death. However, we are only beginning intensive research on the two leading causes of disability in the later years of life: osteoarthritis and Alzheimer's disease. While research on these diseases is relatively recent, at least in the case of Alzheimer's disease, it has been very successful. The identification of specific proteins associated with the brain lesions in this disease led to the localization of a gene for the familial form of Alzheimer's disease to human chromosome 21 (St. George–Hyslop et al., 1987). The same recombinant genetic techniques that helped to make this identification should eventually lead to the isolation of this gene and permit examination of how the abnormal gene leads to the development of Alzheimer's disease.

An important insight into potential interventions in the neurological diseases of aging came through recent work on neuronal cell transplantation in Parkinson's disease (Madrazo et al., 1987). This age-dependent disease is characterized by a loss of specific brain cells in a certain brain region, dopaminergic cells in the substantia nigra. Research in animals with similar conditions revealed that transplantation of these cells from normal animals to affected animals resulted in a return to normal function (Bjorklund et al., 1980). Based on these results and the knowledge that similar dopaminergic cells are present in the adrenal gland, Mexican surgeons recently transplanted adrenal cells from patients with Parkinson's disease to their brains and reduced the symptoms of the disease (Madrazo et al., 1987). Perhaps the most important aspect of the transplantation research is the increasing appreciation of the importance of factors that permit nerve cell growth. While I do not believe that brain cell transplantation will provide the long-term solution for Parkinson's disease or Alzheimer's disease, research in this area may provide us with cell stimulation factors that are specific for the cell populations affected in Parkinson's and Alzheimer's disease.

INTERVENTIONS IN AGING

There are many potential biological, social, and psychological interventions in various aging processes. I would like to present a few examples of potential interventions.

One intriguing intervention on the molecular level is arresting or reversing the glycosylation of proteins, the attachment of glucose (sugar) to proteins. Glycosylation of proteins is occurring constantly, but many of these proteins are short lived and, consequently, the attachment of glucose has little effect. However, there are many proteins that remain in the body for years, and with aging, these proteins become increasingly glycosylated (Cerami, 1986). Glycosylation of proteins makes them susceptible to binding to one another, called cross-linking. The glycosylation and cross-linking of the long-lived lens proteins, the crystallins, may contribute to the age-dependent formation of cataracts. In diabetes, where blood sugar levels are very high, there is increased glycosylation of proteins, which may explain the accelerated formation of cataracts in this disease. It has been proposed that glycosylation and subsequent cross-linking of proteins may play a role in age-dependent renal and cardio-vascular disease (Cerami, 1986). These conditions are also ac-celerated in diabetes. Cerami is examining an intervention to prevent the glycosylation of proteins. Experimental animals are given aminoguanidine and the effect of this agent on collagen, a particularly long-lived protein, is examined (Brownlee et al., 1986). These studies indicate that the formation of glycosylated collagen is significantly prevented. Further research will deter-mine whether this intervention will prevent certain aging proc-esses in these animals.

Another promising area for future interventions is the immune system. This system is the body's front line against infectious agents such as viruses and bacteria. With aging, there is a decline in the function of the immune system, contributing to the in-creased susceptibility of older individuals to life-threatening in-fections such as pneumonia and influenza (Hausman & Weksler, 1985). This age-dependent decline in the function of the immune system is accompanied by the involution of the thymus gland. Hormones secreted by this gland are important for the successful functioning of the cells that comprise the immune system. One potential intervention that is being tried in experimental animals is to give them additional thymic hormones in an attempt to pre-vent this age-dependent decline in immune function. However, the addition of purified thymic hormones does not appear to restore all immune functions (Cowan et al., 1981). Another hor-mone that has an effect on the immune system is interleukin-2, which is produced by the immune cells themselves. Production of this immune hormone appears to decline with aging (Thoman & Weigle, 1982). This hormone is currently being administered to combat certain cancers as well as the acquired immune defi-ciency syndrome (AIDS). In the future, it may be employed as an intervention against the aging of the immune system.

Interventions are not limited to the realm of biomedical geron-tology. One of the most interesting interventions in aging is the psychosocial intervention of giving older individuals control of their environment. Rodin and Langer (1977) took two groups of nursing home residents and let one group control their environment, while the environment of the control group was manipulated for them. As an example, both groups were given plants by the nursing home staff. The experimental group was told that they would have to care for the plants, whereas the staff took care of the plants for the control group. Mortality rates were twice as high in the control group than for the experimental group, and the incidence of various medical conditions was also significantly higher.

CONCLUDING THOUGHTS

Aging research, like other complex research areas, has three stages:

1. A descriptive stage: Scientists attempt to describe the various facets of aging processes.
2. A mechanistic stage: Scientists strive to understand the fundamental nature of various aging processes.
3. An interventive stage: Scientists attempt to alter certain aging processes to extend the healthy years of life.

I believe that aging research is leaving the descriptive stage, is in the midst of the mechanistic stage, and is beginning to consider the interventive stage. It is urgent that we develop interventions soon. If we do not develop them, the diseases and disorders of aging will encompass an increasingly larger proportion of our lifespans. The number of Alzheimer victims will approach 10 million Americans, the number of hip fractures will approach 1 million a year, and the cost of these two conditions will approach $20,000,000,000 in 1985 dollars, a figure higher than the largest deficit of the United States government.

To end on a more positive note: Successful interventions could mean that one could look toward increased numbers of healthy, productive years for all Americans.

REFERENCES

Bjorklund, A., Dunnett, S. B., Stenevi, U., et al. (1980). Reinnervation of the denervated striatum by substantia nigra transplants: Functional consequences as revealed by pharmacological and sensorimotor testing. *Brain Res.*, *199*, 307–333.

Brownlee, M., Vlassara, H., Kooney, A., et al. (1986). Aminoguanidine prevents diabetes-induced arterial wall protein cross-linking. *Science*, *232*, 1629–1632.

Cerami, A. (1986). Aging of proteins and nucleic acids: What is the role of glucose? *Trends in Biochemical Sciences*, *11*, 311–314.

Cowan, M. J., Fujiwara, P., Wara, D. W., et al. (1981). Effect of thymosin on cellular immunity in old age. *Mech. Ag. Develop.*, *15*, 29–39.

Guralnik, J., & Schneider, E. L. (1987). Prospects and implications of extending life expectancy. In T. J. Espenshade & G. J. Stolnitz (Eds.) *Technological Prospects and Population Trends* (pp. 125–146). Boulder, CO: Westview Press.

Hausman, P. B., & Weksler, M. (1985). Changes in the immune response with age. In C. E. Finch & E. L. Schneider (Eds.), *The biology of aging* (2nd ed., pp. 414–432). New York: Van Nostrand Reinhold.

Madrazo, I., Drucker-Colin, R., Diaz, V., et al (1987). Open microsurgical autograft of adrenal medulla to the right caudate nucleus in two patients with intractable Parkinson's disease. *New Engl. J. Med.*, *316*, 831–834.

Rodin, J., & Langer, J. (1977), Long-term effects of a control-relevant intervention. *J. Personaly and Soc. Psychol.*, *35*, 897–902.

Schneider, E. L. & Guralnik, J. (1987). Comprehension of morbidity: A dream which may come true someday. *Gerontologica Biomedica Acta*.

St. George–Hyslop, P. H., Tanzi, R. E., Polinsky, R. J., et al. (1987). The genetic defect causing familial Alzheimer's disease maps on chromosome 21. *Science*, *235*, 885–890.

Thoman, M., & Weigle, W. (1982). Cell-mediated immunity in aged mice: Underlying lesion in IL 2 synthesis. *J. Immunology*, *128*, 2358–2361.

Wilkins, R., & Adams, O. B. (1983). Health expectancy in Canada, late 1970's: Demographic, regional, and social dimensions. *American Journal of Public Health*, *73*, 1073–2080.

New Directions: Oxidized Biopolymers

3

Toru Tsumita

Aging in human beings is accompanied by diverse pathological problems, as well as normal physiological changes. These disease problems and normal changes appear in all biological systems of the body: nervous, vascular, and skeletal. As a consequence, aging theories are quite complex. One simplifying approach is to characterize the fundamental processes that occur before signs of aging appear. Such an analysis may produce helpful practical information.

PHYSIOLOGICAL AGING OR LATENT AGING PROCESS

Taking into account that the human life span is approximately 100 years, signs related to normal processes of aging usually manifest themselves in the latter 50 years. We may ask what happens latently in the first 50 years, the period without such symptoms. As Shock (1972) reported, cross-sectional research on aging has demonstrated that a number of physiological functions begin to decrease after about 20 to 30 years of age (e.g., blood circulation in the heart, kidney, and brain; elasticity of blood vessels and alveoli; hearing and vision abilities). Since

Table 3.1. Human Aging

	Physiological	*Pathological*
Occurrence	Generally	Partly
Beginning	From 20–30 years of age	Not definite
Speed	Slow and steady	Rapid
Treatment	?	Geriatrics

it appears that these changes are followed by aging phenomena in the later life span, they should be designated as physiological or normal aging. Table 3.1 compares two types of human aging processes.

There is another type of age-related change: the age-dependent increase of blood pressure. In this case, the change will be understood as a compensatory or secondary reaction by the host against the decrease in the elasticity of blood vessels. Thus, the decrease of physiological functions occurring just after the end of the growth stage of human life is to be considered as evidence of a primary aging process, as shown in Table 3.2. If we could elucidate the biochemical basis of such early physiological

Table 3.2. Age-Related Change of Biological Activity

Age-Dependent Decrease[a]	*Age-Dependent Increase*[b]
Blood circulation volume: Heart, kidney, brain	Blood pressure
Blood vessel elasticity	
Lung: maximum respiration, alveolar area	Lung: relative duct volume
Immune antibody	Autoimmune antibody
Sex hormones	Noradrenalin
Hearing	Etc.
Vision, etc.	

[a] Primary.
[b] Secondary.

aging, it might be possible to design ways to modify the aging processes that appear in the later life span.

AGING AND METABOLISM
OF BIOPOLYMERS

Most biological molecules that participate in physiological functions are newly synthesized. During functioning *in vivo*, these molecules undergo chemical modification or conformation change. The final products are inactive materials that are excreted or reutilized after hydrolysis. Thus, a living organism maintains a dynamic balance of biosynthesis and destruction, or turnover. In the field of aging research, biopolymers with a very slow turnover rate or no turnover at all are of particular importance. Substances belonging to this group are intracellular connective tissue proteins (like collagen and elastin), lens proteins (like crystallin), and myelin proteins (in nerve tissue). Lefevre and Rucker (1980) reported that once the pool of elastin in the aorta is stabilized as mature fibers, it is not subjected to proteolysis or resynthesis of a sufficient magnitude to result in measurable turnover.

A variety of such "long-life" proteins may be present in *in vivo* tissues, especially in the intracellular matrix. However, due to technical difficulties in measuring proteins having a very long half-life, information on them is quite limited.

In analyzing minor constituents in several kinds of long-life proteins, we have found a very small amount of α-aminoadipic acid δ semialdehyde, which is an oxidized product of lysine at the ε-amino group (Saiot & Tsumita, 1972). The amount was not more than a few moles in 1,000 aminoacid residues. As for collagen and elastin, the same residue has been reported as an oxidized product of lysine residue by lysyl oxidase, which plays a role in the formation of cross-linkages between protein strands (Partridge, Elsden, & Thomas, 1963). The cross-linking thus formed involves desmosine and related compounds. Immature collagen is converted into a mature type. This is an enzyme-regulated physiological reaction. However, it is not reasonable to consider that the same aldehyde found in crystallin (Wada & Tsumita, unpublished), myelin (Wada & Tsumita, 1975), and nucleoprotein (Saiot & Tsumita, 1972) is a product of enzyme-regulated oxidation. It was also reported that the same aldehyde was found in an erythrocyte protein (Langdon, 1974). Similar oxidized residues in proteins seem to increase in a time-dependent manner.

In the case of proteins with an extremely slow turnover rate, it is conceivable that such oxidized residues accumulate in protein molecules so that physical properties of the protein are modified.

Therefore, it seems reasonable to suggest that biopolymers with a slow or no turnover rate are oxidized periodically *in vivo* over a long period of time. Such chemical changes accumulate during several decades of a human's life; extensively modified biopolymers "pull a trigger" for physiological aging.

AGE-DEPENDENT MODIFICATION
OF BIOPOLYMERS

One of the most typical cases is the age-dependent changes of lens proteins. Lens tissues have no blood vessels, and the turnover of lens proteins is almost negligible. Newly formed lens fibers containing crystalline proteins cover the older fiber mass or lens nucleus. Therefore, lens proteins produced in younger years remain in the central portion for a very long period. In addition, photochemical reactions due to ultraviolet and visible light result in the senile cataract, a typical aging phenomenon.

Indeed, many kinds of altered proteins have been reported. Insolubilization or polymerization of crystalline proteins is commonly found with senile and hereditary cataract lenses (Wada, Sugiura, Nakamura, & Tsumita, 1981). Lysine residue of crystallin is partly oxidized. Tryptophane (Dillon, Spector, & Nakanishi, 1976; Van Heyningen, 1973) and tyrosine (Castineiras, Dillon & Spector, 1978) are also oxidized, and the products form colored substances. In addition, it is also reported that L-aspartic acid residue of crystallins is racemized to the D-form at a constant rate of 0.14%, yielding a sort of biological clock (Masters, Bada, & Zigler, 1977).

Of particular interest is the fact that these modifications derive invariably from oxidative reactions. The normal transparent lens of an animal contains a significant amount of reduced low-molecular substances, Vitamin C and glutathione, as well as myoinositol (Wada & Tsumita, 1984), a cyclitol free of a radical scavenger. However, in cataract lenses, the concentration of these compounds is subnormal. Thus, the appearance of oxidized biopolymers and the disappearance of reduced low-molecular substances take place simultaneously in aged cataract lenses. The loss of reducing substances means that active oxygen and free radicals formed by photochemical reactions will not be neutralized. Conceivably, a route is opened to direct oxidation of crystallins. The exact quantifications elude us for now, but the oxidation reduction correlation may stimulate research on finding a defense against the time-dependent aging processes in the lens. As for other tissues, a similar reaction might be occurring, but, due to more active metabolic processes, the situation is not as evident as that of the lens.

LIPID OXIDATION

When polyunsaturated fatty acid is oxidized *in vivo*, the products affect various biopolymers. A typical toxic fragment, malodialdehyde, has been studied, but recent reports show that acrolein derivatives are more toxic. Cholesterol oxide is also toxic. Different from the proteins mentioned above, fatty acid turnover occurs so rapidly that oxidized fatty acids do not accumulate in the lipid moiety. However, reactive fragments derived from oxidation attack other biological components to form various kinds of modified molecules. These affect physiological function. Such modified molecules can have mutagenic, cytotoxic, and carcinogenic actions, as shown in Table 3.3.

Table 3.3. Effect of Oxidized Lipid on Biopolymers

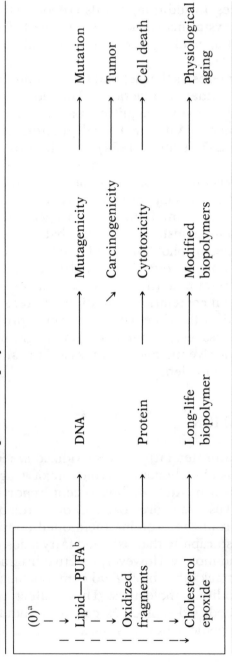

$(O)^a$

Lipid—PUFA^b $\longrightarrow$ DNA $\longrightarrow$ Mutagenicity $\longrightarrow$ Mutation

Oxidized fragments $\nearrow$ Carcinogenicity $\longrightarrow$ Tumor

$\longrightarrow$ Protein $\longrightarrow$ Cytotoxicity $\longrightarrow$ Cell death

Cholesterol epoxide $\longrightarrow$ Long-life biopolymer $\longrightarrow$ Modified biopolymers $\longrightarrow$ Physiological aging

^{a} (O): active type of oxygen.
^{b} PUFA: polyunsaturated fatty acids.

A REVIEW ON AGING THEORIES

Many theories on aging have been proposed (Table 3.4). Each theory seems to be based on experimental results. However, none is able to cover the wide range of aging phenomena. From a biological perspective, I would like to classify them tentatively into four groups.

Group I: Theories dealing with bioactive substances responsible for the modification or denaturation of biopolymers. Active types of oxygen and free radicals are the main concern.

Group II: Theories in which modified biopolymers are considered to be responsible for harmful biological reactions. Accumulation of these altered biopolymers may disturb the normal function of organs. For example, modification of DNA might express somatic mutation, and that of enzyme proteins might express error in biosynthesis.

Group III: Theories of aging due to time-dependent decrease of organ activity, that is, decreases seen in endocrine organs, neurotransmitters in nervous tissue, immunoactive organs or cells, and at multi-organ levels of an organism's functioning.

Group IV: Theories dealing with preset (genetic) programs for aging, through which various aging processes take place sequentially.

This classification is, of course, not definitive but may help us in considering how to modify overall patterns of aging through countermeasures suited to each group of phenomena.

The research focus based on the first group would be on so-called scavenger systems that neutralize the toxicity of active oxygen and free radicals. Cutler (1985) has suggested that longevity of animals depends on the activity of such scavenger systems.

With regard to the second group, immune systems and especially phagocytic systems would be investigated, to find out how to facilitate removal of denatured biopolymers formed in processes of aging.

Table 3.4. Theories on Animal Aging

	Group I	Group II	Group III	Group IV
	Reactant/ Oxidizer	*Modified Biopolymer*	*Functional Decrease*	*Aging Program*
A[a]	Active oxygen	Waste product	Endocrine	Program
	Free radicals	X-linking	Neurotransmitter	Biological clock
		Wear and tear	Immune cells	Metabolism rate
		Somatic mutation (DNA)	Regulatory system	
		Error (enzyme)	Stress (multi-organ)	
B[b]	Scavenge system	Biological clearance (phagocyte system)	Drugs, hormones	

[a] A: aging theories.
[b] B: conceivable countermeasure.

The host must be able to remove metabolic waste products or aged cells in order to maintain functional capacities. Against the exogenous biopolymers of pathogens, animals activate the immune process. The host's macrophages and phagocytic cells achieve elimination via serial processes, that is, recognition, phagocytosis, and hydrolysis. Research on physiological aging requires us to find an effective assay for the activity of phagocytic systems.

As for the third group, involving the age-dependent decrease of organ activity, an exogenous supply of hormones or drugs may be all that is necessary to restore function. Thus, when effective treatments are found, they can become part of geriatric therapy.

The principal approach to modifying the overall pattern of host aging may be based on animals' defense systems, to investigate how the scavenger and phagocytic systems might be protected and made more effective.

SUMMARY

Physiological aging seems to take place in a latent form after the end of the growth stage of human life. During that long period, highly stable biopolymers are oxidized or modified *in vivo* by an active form of oxygen and free radicals derived from lipid oxidation. Such chemical changes increase in a time-dependent manner and affect the physiological function of biopolymers. Thus, extensively modified biopolymers induce physiological aging. Against such time-dependent changes, animals—including human beings—have scavenger and clearance functions. Potentially, this defense system might be an important approach for affecting the aging process.

REFERENCES

Castineiras, S. G., Dillon, J., & Spector, A. (1978). *Science, 199*, 897.
Cutler, R. G. (1985). Peroxide-producing potential of tissues: Inverse correlation with longevity mammalian species. *Proc. Natl. Acad. Sci.—USA, 82*, 4798–4802.

Dillon, J., Spector, A., & Nakanishi, K. (1976). Identification of beta carbolines isolated from flourescent human lens proteins. *Nature, 259*, 422–423.

Langdon, R. G. (1974). Lysine-derived crosslinks in the proteins of the human erythrocyte membrane. *Biochim. Biophys. Acta., 342*, 229–236.

Lefevre, M., & Rucker, R. B. (1980). Aorta elastin turnover in normal and hypercholesterolemic Japanese qual. *Biochim. Biophys. Acta., 630*, 519–529.

Masters, P. M., Bada, J. L., & Zigler, J. S., Jr. (1977). Aspartic acid racemisation in the human lens during aging and in cataract formation. *Nature, 268*, 71–73.

Partridge, S. M., Elsden, D. F., & Thomas, J. (1963). Constitution of the cross-linkages in elastin. *Nature, 197*, 1297–1298.

Saiot, M., & Tsumita, T. (1972). *Japan J. Exp. Med., 42*, 389.

Shock, N. W. (1972). In Carson, L. A. (Ed.), *Nutrition in old age*. X Symposium Swedish Nutrition Foundation, Uppsala, Sweden: Almquist & Wiksel.

Van Heyningen, R. (1973). Assay of flourescent glucosides in the human lens. *Exp. Eye Res., 17*, 121–126.

Wada, E., Sugiura, T., Nakamura, H., & Tsumita, T. (1981). Studies on lens proteins of mice with hereditary cataract. *Biochim. Biophys. Acta., 667*, 251–259.

Wada, E., & Tsumita, T., unpublished manuscript.

Wada, E., & Tsumita, T. (1975). *Japan J. Exp. Med., 45*, 313.

Wada, E., & Tsumita, T. (1984). *Mechanism of Aging and Development, 27*, 287.

Work Ability in
Later Life

II

Introduction to Part II

Having delved into basic processes of aging in Part I, the conference turned next to issues of performance and aging. The contributors furnish a rich scientific arsenal for dealing with age prejudice. For example, Dr. Shigenobu Nakamura and Dr. Carl Cotman emphasize that the nervous system, once thought fated to functional decline, has enduring capacities to adapt and compensate for age-related losses and diseases. The brain possesses plasticity, and this ability may be stimulated.

Among other points, Dr. John Rowe, a physiologist, notes the diversity of the elderly population and patterns of life in old age. He asks if this diversity is not informing us of the plasticity of aging: Not only is "aging" not a rigid pattern of deterioration, as the stereotype holds, but there are subsets of older people whose patterns may be classified as "successful" and as "usual" patterns. The former is marked by less deterioration and greater control over socioenvironmental factors. These individuals should be studied to discover reasons for their achievements. Some of these reasons appear to lie with life-style, including exercise, diet, and general activity. From the perspective of performance, the message again is that aging is malleable.

Dr. James Birren, a psychologist, indicates that investigations in psychology (as well as in other sciences) are only beginning to redress their perspectives on aging. In the past, there was an overemphasis on deficit states, and this reinforced age prejudice and the dismissal of the productive potential (and thereby the suppression of that capacity) of older people. Dr. Birren shows us how older people, as workers and family members, often possess social skills, technical skills, values (such as a concern for quality of work), and wisdom not ordinarily found in younger adults at all or to the same degree. They may possess special kinds of creativity based on experience and insight. Science needs to develop ways to measure these capacities, find their relationship to behavior and performance, and help design environments and other arrangements that promote productivity and satisfaction with life. Dr. Birren offers policymakers a key reference to a study suggesting that occupation more than age determines when people die and the cause. In such ways, science opens up areas for policy consideration typically foreclosed by age prejudice. Policy should turn on facts, not prejudice.

Part II builds toward a question that leaders in public and industrial policy might ponder in depth: The characteristics of an aging population are shaped in major ways by concepts, prejudices, and ignorance. As Dr. Butler observed, ". . . productivity is essential to human health. Without providing an opportunity to be productive, we condemn the human being to becoming dysfunctional. . . ." What we have called the inescapable deterioration of aging has more to do with changeable conditions of life than we heretofore appreciated. "Productive aging" is no oxymoron.

Physiologic Condition and Physical Performance in Older Persons

4

John W. Rowe

This paper reviews available information regarding the physiologic changes that occur in aging humans and their physical capacities.

PHYSIOLOGIC CHANGES WITH AGING

Studies of the capacities of older persons begin by facing the issue of definition of a "normal" aging population. Investigators involved in such studies have, from the beginning, recognized the importance of identifying and excluding individuals in whom the effects of specific diseases might confound the pure effects of aging. Thus, for physiologic studies, careful guidelines are generally developed to exclude individuals whose age-determined responses might be contaminated by specific disease processes. Results in the population remaining after such exclusions have generally been interpreted as representing "normal" aging, especially when the data came from longitudinal studies rather than cross-sectional comparisons of different age groups (Andres, 1985; Rowe, 1977; Shock et al., 1984).

Over the past several years substantial information has become available to suggest that this differentiation into "normal" and diseased elderly falls short of the proper stratification of the population for studies of the aging process. The concept of "normal" aging has several weaknesses including its neglect of the heterogeneity of the physiologic changes with age; its implication that the "normal" changes associated with aging are harmless and carry no risk; and lastly, the implication that "normal" changes are somehow natural and thus beyond the scope of purposeful modification (Shock et al., 1984).

Review of the physiologic changes that occur in humans as they age allows development of several principles of clinical gerontology (Andres, 1985). The first consideration that emerges is that of the phases of the normal lifespan. The early phase of growth and development, which is characterized by rapid increases in many functions, generally continues into early adulthood, peaking in the late 20s or 30s. In those variables that do change with age after adulthood, the change generally begins immediately at the end of the growth and development phase and is generally linear into old age. In most cases there is no pleasant plateau of the middle years in which one maintains function at a prime level. Thus, the rate of aging does not change in groups as they age. While an 80-year-old is more aged than a 30-year-old, having accumulated more of the changes secondary to age, he or she is not losing function at a more rapid rate.

Another characteristic of the physiology of aging is that changes in one organ are not necessarily predictive of changes with age in other organs. If an apparently healthy 60-year-old is found on serial prospective measurements to have pulmonary function that is declining at a certain rate, this information is not of particular assistance in predicting the rate at which her or his kidneys, thyroid, sympathetic nervous system, or any other organ might change over time.

An important characteristic of age-related changes is their variability. In almost all data sets of factors that change significantly with age one can find older individuals who perform at or above the level of the average younger individual. Although the sources of this variability have been unclear to date, increasing evidence, as is discussed below, points to factors extrinsic to the aging process per se.

In view of the drawbacks of the term "normal aging," and the accumulating data suggesting that factors extrinsic to the aging process may account for the often dramatic variability within the nondiseased aging population, it has recently been suggested that the "normal" nondiseased aged population might be viewed as containing two general subsets: a successfully aging subset in which the effects of extrinsic factors are minimal and in which aging effects alone persist, often resulting in quite modest reductions when compared with healthy younger individuals; and a "usual" aging group, in which the effects of pure aging are complicated and magnified by concurrent effects of extrinsic factors (Rowe & Kahn, 1987). As the various extrinsic factors that might complicate age-determined changes in various organs are identified, increasingly robust studies will be performed to identify the effects of the intrinsic aging process.

As noted above, numerous cross-sectional and longitudinal studies indicate the general decline in a number of important organs and organ systems with age. While most of these studies have not differentiated between the successful and usual subsets of aging, having lumped together all nondiseased populations, they have identified marked age-related changes in a number of important physiologic factors including hearing, vision, renal function, glucose tolerance, regulation of the volume and composition of the extracellular fluid, maintenance of blood pressure under stress, bone density, pulmonary function, immune function, and sympathetic nervous system function.

For many of these variables, between the ages of 30 and 80, reductions of between 15 and 60% of function can be seen. However, given the substantial physiological reserve of most if not all organs, the clinical effects of these age-related changes are generally modest if at all discernible under basal circumstances. The major impact of the physiology of aging is not in altering basal function; that is, the normal older individual has adequate lung function to avoid being short of breath under normal circumstances, has adequate renal function to maintain normal volume and composition of the extracellular fluid, has adequate physiologic sympathetic function to maintain normal blood pressure and body temperature, and so forth. The major effects of these age-related changes is unveiled under stress, either environmental or associated with acute or chronic illness, during which time the physiologic repertoire of the older individual is substantially constrained compared with that of his younger counterpart. Thus, as pointed out by Weksler, the normal homeostasis that characterizes physiologic systems in youth is replaced by "homeostenosis": a constricted physiologic capacity to respond to stress.

Perhaps an example of the clinical influence of this constricted homeostasis would be helpful. Imagine an 80-year-old individual and his 30-year-old grandson. Both acquire acute pneumococcal pneumonia in their right lower lobes. If, before the infection, each of these individuals has physiologic pulmonary functional capacity similar to that of the average individual of his age group, the impact of the acute illness will be strikingly different in the two individuals. The young patient may be febrile for several days but will not be likely to require hospitalization, will respond promptly to appropriate antibiotics, and be back to work in a week. The grandfather, on the other hand, is at much greater risk for requiring hospitalization and perhaps even for succumbing to this illness. This is related not so much to a difference in the specific illness which he develops (i.e., infecting organism, lobe of lung, etc.) but rather to his limited physiologic reserve in terms of both pulmonary and immune function, limiting his capacity to prevent the development of sepsis.

Specific Physiologic Changes with Age

The specific physiologic changes that occur with advancing age in several organs will be reviewed in order to provide greater insight into the physiology of aging.

Cardiac Function at Rest

The physical examination of the heart is not necessarily altered with age, although nonradiating systolic ejection murmurs, generally attributed to aortic sclerosis, are common over age 75.

The electrocardiogram is also generally not importantly changed with age in the absence of disease.

There is no effect of advancing age on cardiac output (the amount of blood pumped per minute) in the sitting position, but there is a modest decline when lying supine. This suggests that older persons do not increase their cardiac output in response to the increased preload associated with the supine position as much as their younger counterparts.

Important aspects of heart function at rest not influenced by age include the width of the left ventricle (the major chamber of the heart), as well as its volume and ejection fraction (the portion of blood it ejects with each beat). Basal heart rate declines modestly with age and is compensated for by a slight increase in stroke volume to maintain cardiac output. There is no change in peripheral resistance with age, despite a slight increase in systolic blood pressure. Left-ventricular wall thickness increases with age, probably secondary to the increased work it undergoes because of the age-related increase in systolic blood pressure.

An important change with age is the decline in the capacity of the heart to relax (diastolic filling), which is probably due to age-related prolongation of isometric relaxation time and decreases in cardiac compliance secondary to collagen accumulation in the ventricle. Thus, as the ventricle stiffens with age, relaxation is impaired and filling slows. This becomes important when heart rate is increased and relaxation time (diastole) shortens, leading to inadequate filling, pulmonary venous congestion, and shortness of breath (Weisfeldt, Gerstenblith, & Lakatta, 1985).

Cardiac Performance Under Stress

At various levels of exercise, cardiac output rises in older individuals to similar levels as seen in their younger counterparts. Since maximal heart rate during exercise declines with age, cardiac output is maintained via an increase in stroke volume and left-ventricular end diastolic volume. Although left-ventricular ejection fraction declines with age, the absolute amount of blood ejected with each contraction is greater in the elderly, since left-ventricular end diastolic volume is clearly increased, and thus an adequate stroke volume can be maintained at a lower ejection fraction.

In summary, the senescent human heart is fully capable of maintaining adequate overall function, that is, cardiac output, both under basal circumstances and in response to stress. Specific physiologic effects of aging, primarily related to decreased compliance of the left ventricle and impaired diastolic function as well as impaired chronotropic response to stress, lead to specific adaptations. Thus, adequate cardiac output is maintained during exercise via increases in left-ventricular end diastolic volume and stroke volume to compensate for the lack of increase in cardiac output. These physiologic changes are important clinically since they may explain the tendency of older individuals to develop pulmonary venous congestion during uncontrolled atrial fibrillation or other forms of supraventricular tachycardia and also help to explain the blunted response of the elderly to beta-adrenergic agonist and antagonist stimulation. Clearly, heart function in normal older persons is adequate to support the demands associated with moderate or even more strenuous exercise.

Carbohydrate Metabolism

An age-related impairment in the capacity to maintain normal blood sugar (glucose) levels after glucose challenge has been recognized for over 60 years (Davidson, 1979). Increasing age in individuals without clinical evidence or family history of diabetes is associated with a progressive decline in the capacity to metabolize glucose, including a slight (1 mg/dl/decade) increase after maturity in fasting blood glucose levels, and rather striking increases in blood sugar after oral glucose challenge averaging 8 to 10 mg/dl/decade at 1 hour. Recent studies indicate that at least 22% of Americans aged 65 to 74 demonstrate impaired carbohydrate tolerance that is not severe enough to warrant a diagnosis of diabetes mellitus (Meneilly, Greenspan, Rowe, & Minaker, 1988). The increases in postprandial glucose levels seen with aging are also reflected in increased levels of hemoglobin AlC with age.

Pathogenic mechanisms postulated to explain these changes in carbohydrate tolerance include age-related changes in body composition, diet, activity, and insulin secretion and action. Marked limitation of physical activity and administration of diets low in carbohydrate content will impair glucose tolerance. Age-associated changes in body composition may play an important role in determining age effects in carbohydrate metabolism. In response to oral or intravenous glucose challenges, elderly on high carbohydrate intakes have repeatedly been found to have circulating insulin levels that are equivalent to, or in many cases greater than, levels found in their younger counterparts. Thus, the major effect of age under these conditions is decrease of the effectiveness of insulin to induce glucose metabolism in peripheral tissues (Minaker, Meneilly, & Rowe, 1984). It appears that the insulin resistance of aging is due to a defect in transport of sugar into cells. On diets low in carbohydrate content, older persons demonstrate impaired insulin release as well as insulin resistance.

The carbohydrate intolerance of aging may carry substantial risk. According to a recent report from the Honolulu Heart Study, in nondiabetics, the risk of stroke is moderately age related and was statistically significantly higher for those at the 80th percentile serum glucose when compared with those at the 20th percentile. Also, studies focusing on postprandial hyperinsulinemia, a cardinal feature of the insulin resistance of aging, have shown increases in insulin levels to be a significant independent contributor to the incidence of coronary artery disease (Abbott et al., 1987).

Although the glucose intolerance of aging is common and clearly associated with an increased risk of vascular disease, there is no evidence at present that treatment of glucose intolerance, as opposed to frank diabetes, will decrease the risk of these complications. Nonetheless, it would be prudent to recommend moderate exercise and weight loss to older individuals with greater degrees of glucose intolerance.

The initial sections of this chapter outlined the rationale for stratifying nondiseased age-related changes into those associated with intrinsic aging per se and those associated with extrinsic factors. With this perspective in mind, it is interesting to note that several recent attempts have been made to determine which components of the age-associated alterations in carbohydrate tolerance are related to aging per se and which might be related to factors such as diet, exercise, medications, and body composition. For example, in Italian factory workers aged 22 to 73 years, Zavaroni and co-workers (1986) evaluated the relative contributions of obesity, physical activity, family history of diabetes, and the use of diabetogenic drugs to age-related increases in glucose and insulin levels after an oral glucose tolerance test. The initial strong statistical correlation between age and both postprandial glucose and insulin levels became much weaker when the effects of exercise, diet, and drugs were taken into account, so that the correlation between glucose and age was limited to marginal statistical significance and there was no longer an effect of age on insulin levels. Hollenbeck and co-workers (1985) showed a direct and statistically significant relationship between physical fitness as reflected in maximal oxygen consumption and insulin-stimulated glucose metabolism in nonobese healthy older men. Additionally, Seals and co-workers (1984) found that performance of older physically trained men on oral glucose tolerance tests was identical to that of young athletes and significantly better than that of untrained older men.

Renal Function

With the possible exceptions of pulmonary and immune function, the changes in kidney function with normal aging are the most dramatic of any human organ or organ system. In a normal young adult, renal capacity far exceeds the ordinary demands for solute and water conservation and excretion. In old age, renal function, while substantially diminished, still provides under ordinary circumstances for adequate regulation of the volume and composition of extracellular fluid. However, the reduced function of the aged kidney has important clinical implications for diagnosis and treatment of many disorders and clearly reduces the individual's capacity to respond to a variety of physiological and pathological stresses.

The major clinically relevant functional defect in the kidneys with age is a progressive decline after maturity in the glomerular filtration rate. Age-adjusted normative standards for kidney function have recently been established. Creatinine clearance is stable until the middle of the fourth decade when a linear decrease of about 7% per decade begins. As was mentioned above in the care of cardiac function, the losses in kidney function with normal aging do not influence the capacity of the elderly to cope with moderate or even more strenuous physical exercise. However, these age-related declines are important in the presence of acute or chronic illness, or administration of medications, which are excreted via kidney function (Rowe, 1985).

It is of particular interest that recent studies have provided some insight into the substantial variability in renal change with age. As noted before, many physiologic changes associated with aging show marked interindividual variability, and this is certainly the case with regard to renal function. While individuals who had any one of a number of diseases that might be associated with impairment of renal function were excluded from the studies outlined above, there was still substantial variability in the creatinine clearances of the oldest group, with many old individuals demonstrating renal function similar to that of the average young individual. Detailed studies of this same study population by Lindeman, Tobin, and Shock (1985) have shown a statistically significant inverse relationship between increases in systolic blood pressure below the hypertensive range and progressive reductions in renal function. Clearly, the increases in systolic pressure associated with aging may be related to increases in fatness as well as other variables not related to intrinsic aging per se.

EFFECTS OF INTERVENTIONS ON REVERSING PHYSIOLOGIC CHANGES WITH AGE

Implicit in the differentiation of age-*associated* changes into age-*determined* effects of the intrinsic aging process and age-*related* effects of extrinsic or environmental factors is the suggestion that the extrinsic component may in fact be preventable or reversible. An example of the possible beneficial effects of interventions on the extrinsic component of what has previously been considered "normal" aging can be seen in the case of exercise. Exercise has been shown to enhance cardiovascular function, oxygen consumption, sugar metabolism, and bone density in elderly individuals, thus reversing the extrinsic component of "normal" age changes in four different systems, suggesting the substantial plasticity or modifiability of what was previously considered to be immutable age-related changes.

Maximum oxygen consumption is generally considered the gold standard of physical fitness. A number of studies have shown that the oxygen consumption capacity of older individuals can be substantially enhanced through a program of regular exercise and that the oxygen consumption capacity of trained older individuals not only is greater than that of older sedentary individuals but can in fact exceed that of younger sedentary individuals (Wei & Gersh, 1987). With regard to the sugar metabolism capacity of the elderly, which is discussed in detail above, as noted previously, several studies have shown a statistically significant relation between physical fitness as reflected in maximum oxygen consumption and insulin-stimulated glucose metabolism in healthy older men (Hollenbeck, et al., 1985; Seals et al., 1984).

In addition, at least two recent studies have indicated that exercise programs can improve the sugar metabolism of older individuals (Seals, Hagberg, Hurley, Ehsani, & Holloszy, 1984; Tonino, Nedde, Robbins, & Horton, 1986). It is also well known that aging is associated with a progressive decline in bone density in both males and females after maturity. Losses in bone density so severe as to result in fractures after minimal trauma define the "disease" osteoporosis, which accounts for more than 1 million fractures in the United States each year. Those individuals at greatest risk are the most elderly white females. It is of substantial interest that a number of recent studies have shown that regular exercise even among very old women can result in a blunting, if not a complete cessation, of previous age-related bone loss (Shock et al., 1984).

With regard to cardiovascular changes and exercise training, several studies in animals have shown that the aged cardiovascular system can adapt to exercise conditioning with significant improvement in its function. Studies comparing older sedentary humans with their consistently exercising counterparts show that those who exercise have maximum oxygen uptake approximately 10% higher than those who do not. Physically conditioned older persons also have lower body fat, lower blood pressure, and lower resting heart rate than old sedentary persons (Wei & Gersh, 1987).

Thus, it can be seen with regard to this one intervention—exercise—that substantive changes can occur in cardiovascular and pulmonary function and carbohydrate and bone metabolism, all areas previously assumed to be immutable age-related losses. Data of this sort lead to substantial optimism as to the possibility of intervention strategies substantially improving the status of the elderly.

PHYSICAL PERFORMANCE
OF OLDER PERSONS

Until recently, studies of the physical performance of older persons focused on minimal levels of function, such as evaluation of an individual's capacities with regard to the Activities of Daily Living Scale of Katz (Katz & Akpon, 1976). This widely used scale includes items regarding capacity and independence in self-care, including bathing, grooming, dressing, eating, toileting, and transferring from bed to chair. Such an approach, while critical in determining the clinical needs of frail elders, identifies only those who are markedly impaired, lumping the remaining overwhelming majority into a nonimpaired group, and tells us little about the physical capacity of nonfrail elders. The Katz ADL scale is often supplemented by the Instrumental ADL scale, which includes items such as shopping, transportation, managing finances, and the like. Though an additional aid in planning clinical services, this still falls far short of evaluating physical capacity of the majority of elders.

Increasingly, measures of more taxing physical capacities are being included in studies of the elderly. The two most frequently used measures are the Rosow-Breslau (Rosow & Breslau, 1966) and the Nagi (Nagi, 1976) scales. The Rosow-Breslau scale seeks to identify gross mobility limitations. A modification of this scale including three items, that is, capacity to perform heavy housework, ability to walk up and down a flight of stairs, and to walk a half mile, has recently been applied in the coordinated multisite NIA-supported Established Populations for the Epidemiologic Study of the Elderly (EPESE). These studies include detailed evaluation of well-characterized community-living elderly populations in East Boston, New Haven, and Iowa.

In New Haven, which is representative of the entire study, these studies identified a remarkable degree of physical fitness in the elderly (Foley, Berkman, Branch, Farmer, & Wallace, 1986). The proportion of elderly men able to perform all of the three listed activities was 75% between the ages of 65 and 74, 59% between 75 and 84, and down to 42% above age 85. Similarly, functional levels for elderly women, though somewhat lower than those seen in the men, were still high. Sixty-six percent of women age 65 to 74 were able to perform all three activities, a proportion that fell to 44% between ages 75 and 84, and 19% after age 85.

An additional approach to estimating physical function is represented by the Nagi scale, which includes five items of physical capacity: pushing and pulling large objects, such as a living room chair; stooping, crouching, and kneeling; lifting weights less than 10 pounds; reaching over shoulder level; and writing or handling small objects. These measures have also been included in the EPESE, and again citing the New Haven results, 74% of men age 65 to 74 reported no disability with regard to these measures. This portion of high-performing men declines slowly to 63% over age 85. As with the Rosow-Breslau scale, women perform slightly less well, with 60% showing no disability at age 65 to 74, and 34% showing at least one reported disability after age 85.

This emerging picture of a physically capable, active elderly population gains further support from the recent studies of Guralnik (1985), from the Human Population Laboratory Aging

Study, based in Alameda County, California. In 1984, he conducted a telephone survey of a cohort of individuals born prior to 1920 who were enrolled in the Alameda County study, and he determined their capacity to perform a variety of measures of strenuous activity and vigorous exercise. Regarding strenuous activities—heavy housework, moving large objects, lifting or carrying over 10 pounds—Guralnik found that 62% of those over age 65 were able to perform these activities. By this criterion, the proportion of physically fit people was stable, near 65 to 70% up to age 79, falling off dramatically thereafter to a low of 21% over the age of 85. Regarding exercise, such as gardening, camping, hunting, fishing, swimming, jogging, calisthenics, aerobics, bicycling, tennis, and the like, Guralnik again found a very high fitness proportion. Approximately 90% up until age 79 engaged in at least one of these activities, with a gradual falloff to 61% over age 85. Pushing the issue even further and inquiring as to what portion of the elderly were able to engage in these activities often, he found that up to age 84 over 60% of the individuals did so. Looking at even more vigorous exercises, that is, working up a sweat while jogging, doing aerobics, hiking, and so on, at least weekly, participation rates remained over 70% up until age 79. The physically elite elderly, that is, those often participating in such vigorous activities, comprised 20% up to age 74, and then fell gradually to 15% up to age 84, and 2.3% thereafter.

Taken together, these results provide substantial insight into the actual physical capacities of our rapidly growing elderly population. For decades, "ageism" has led us to the view that the elderly are frail and incapacitated, need our help, and are unable to participate in demanding physical work. Clearly, that is not the case. As can be seen from the data reviewed in this chapter, exercise not only has beneficial effects on limiting the physiologic changes that occur with age but is also a health-promotion, disease-prevention mechanism that is easily within the reach of most elders. Additionally, it is time we recognized that the rapidly growing population of elderly individuals is generally physically fit and represents a possible resource for enhanced productivity, which would benefit society as well as the elderly themselves.

The author is grateful for the assistance of Drs. Jack Guralnik and Teresa Seeman. This work was supported by the MacArthur Foundation Research Program on Successful Aging.

REFERENCES

Abbott, R. D., et al. (1987). Diabetes and the risk of stroke. *Journal of the American Medical Association, 257,* 949.

Andres, R. A. (1985). Normal aging versus disease in the elderly. In R. Andres, E. L. Bierman, & W. Hazzard (Eds.), *Principles of geriatric medicine* (p. 38). New York: McGraw-Hill.

Davidson, M. B. (1979). The effect of aging on carbohydrate metabolism: A review of the English literature and a practical approach to the diagnosis of diabetes mellitus in the elderly. *Metabolism, 28,* 688.

Foley, D. J., Berkman, L. F., Branch, L. G., Farmer, M. E., & Wallace, R. B. (1986). Physical functioning. In J. Cormoni-Huntley, D. B. Brock, A. M. Ostfeld, J. O. Taylor, & R. B. Wallace (Eds.), *Established populations for epidemiologic studies of the elderly* (resource data book, pp. 56–94). National Institute on Aging (U.S. DHHS-NIH Publication No. 86-2443). Washington, DC: U.S. Government Printing Office.

Guralnik, J. M. (1985). Determinants of functional health status in the elderly. Unpublished doctoral dissertation, Department of Epidemiology, University of California, Berkeley.

Hollenbeck, C. B., Haskell, W., Rosenthal, M., & Reaven, G. M. (1985). *Journal of the American Geriatric Association, 33,* 273.

Katz, S., & Akpon, C. A. (1976). A measure of primary sociological functions. *International Journal of Health Services, 6,* 493.

Lindeman, R. D., Tobin, J. D., & Shock, N. W. (1985). Longitudinal studies on the rate of decline in renal function with age. *Journal of the American Geriatrics Society, 33,* 278.

Meneilly, G. S., Greenspan, S. L., Rowe, J. W., & Minaker, K. L. (1988). Endocrine systems. In *Geriatric Medicine.* Boston: Little, Brown.

Minaker, K. L., Meneilly, G. S., & Rowe, J. W. (1984). Endocrinology of aging. In C. Finch & E. Schneider (Eds.), *Handbook of the biology of aging* (pp. 433–456). New York: Van Nostrand Reinhold.

Nagi, S. Z. (1976). An epidemiology of disability among adults in the United States. *Milbank Memorial Fund Quarterly, 54,* 439.

Rosow, I., & Breslau, W. (1966). A Guttman health scale for the aged. *Journal of Gerontology, 21,* 556.

Rowe, J. W. (1977). Clinical research in aging: Strategies and directions. *New England Journal of Medicine, 297,* 1332–1336.

Rowe, J. W. (1985). Alterations in renal function. In R. A. Andres, E. L. Bierman, & W. H. Hazzard (Eds.), *Principles of geriatric medicine* (pp. 319–324). New York: McGraw-Hill.

Rowe, J. W., & Kahn, R. L. (1987). Human aging: Usual and successful. *Science, 237,* 143–149.

Seals, D. L., Hagberg, J. M., Allen, W. K., Hurley, B. F., Dalsky, G. P., Ehsani, A. A., & Holloszy, J. O. (1984). Glucose tolerance in young and older athletes and sedentary men. *Journal of Applied Physiology, 56,* 1521.

Seals, D. L., Hagberg, J. M., Hurley, B. F., Ehsani, A. A., & Holloszy, J. O. (1984). Effects of endurance training on glucose tolerance and plasma lipid levels in older men and women. *Journal of the American Medical Association, 252,* 645.

Shock, N. W., et al. (1984). Normal human aging. *The Baltimore longitudinal study of aging.* Washington, DC: U.S. Department of Health & Human Services.

Tonino, R. P., Nedde, W. H., Robbins, D. C., & Horton, E. S. (1986). Effect of physical training on the insulin resistance of aging. *Clinical Research, 34,* 557.

Wei, J. Y., & Gersh, B. J. (1987). Heart disease in the elderly. *Current Problems in Cardiovascular Disease, 12,* 65.

Weisfeldt, M. L., Gerstenblith, G., & Lakatta, E. G. (1985). Alterations in circulatory function. In R. Andres, E. L. Bierman, & W. Hazzard (Eds.), *Principles of geriatric medicine* (p. 248). New York: McGraw-Hill.

Zavaroni, I., et al. (1986). Effect of age and environmental factors on glucose tolerance and insulin secretion in a worker population. *Journal of the American Geriatric Society, 34,* 271.

Measuring Our Psychological Performance

5

James E. Birren
and
Marion A. Perlmutter

BACKGROUND

There are two faces of aging. One face is optimistic since more of us are living longer and are better educated and more competent than ever before. The second face is less pleasant, for it shows a large number of older persons who are ill, may be physically and psychologically disabled, and may live in impoverished circumstances. We must recognize these two faces of later life and respond to their implications. We have to live with this dual perspective and not substitute the simple stereotype that growing old is wholly an "upper" or a "downer"; it is both, and our measurements should embrace all aspects. Here we are looking at ways to measure our productivity and potentials, the complement to the losses some experience with advancing age.

We want to develop a guide to measuring our psychological capacities over the adult life span. In these last years of the 20th century, new questions arise about the increased life expectancy and the aging demographic profile of America. We are older, retiring earlier, tending to live alone, and more likely to be female than male (Pifer & Bronte, 1986). But there are more competent, healthy, and potentially productive mature persons in America than ever in our history. This picture gives rise to challenging scientific questions. A few are listed here:

48

What are the capacities of older adults that can be mobilized for their well-being and that of society?

How can society utilize the productive potential of adults in the third and fourth quarters of life?

What are the key psychological and social factors that enhance or impair successful aging and good mental health in the second half of life?

What are the biological, psychological, and social factors that lead to successful adaptation to life circumstances and competence in late life?

What relationship does the gap between female and male life expectancy have to differences between men and women in health behavior, stress, and coping resources?

What are the life-styles that maintain health and productivity in the later years?

As a science, psychology sits in between the biomedical and social sciences. Because of this position, psychology has had to incorporate some of the perspectives of these fields as it does research to answer questions, such as those listed above, about the competence and productivity of mature and elderly adults. Assisting our search for new knowledge is the growth in computer capacity and our skills for designing complex research. We have begun to examine the mutual influences of health, the environment, and beliefs and behaviors in the processes of aging. We have entered a new era of measurement that may contribute to the utilization of resources in our older populations.

HUMAN RESOURCES

There is evidence that as successive generations have marched through our nation's school systems, aspects of their intellectual capacity have increased (Labouvie-Vief, 1985). Put simply, many adults of today know more than their counterparts of several generations ago. Thus, the brain does not appear as a fixed memory capacity system, but as one that has much unused potential for the storage of information. This may be put in perspective by noting that the average college graduate has about half the vocabulary size that he or she will have at age 65. Starting out with a good education and being exposed to information over the course of adult life lead to a vocabulary size of about 45,000 words in late adult life, in contrast to approximately 22,000 words at the point of leaving college (Seashore & Eckerson, 1940). The healthy older brain continues to gain information. Furthermore, after 30 to 40 years of age, individuals have gained many technical and social skills.

Resources may be increasing with age in an era when we are retiring earlier, creating a paradox. Just as developed countries cannot afford to neglect the development and use of intelligence in their young, they cannot neglect to develop and utilize the intelligence, experience, and productivity of their older populations. To date, psychologists have been much concerned with the measurement of deficit states and the consequences of diseases associated with age. We are becoming expert in the measurement of deficit states and the generation of knowledge about persons who have defects of a genetic nature, are at high risk for particular diseases, or suffer the consequences of self-destructive behavior such as substance abuse. In this sense, we know more about downward mobility in our society, economically and behaviorally, than we do about upward mobility.

However, since we cannot afford to neglect the resources that exist in older persons, psychologists must also develop the capacity to identify and measure this potential. As a humane society we must use knowledge and resources to prevent and alleviate human limitations and misery, but we must also encourage research that helps us become more expert in understanding the pathways to becoming vigorous and healthy mature adults and the pathways to high-level accomplishment. We must be able to assess ripe or mature talents, talents that can be nourished and encouraged toward high-level accomplishments in the sciences, arts, and human services.

One reason for the gap in knowledge about late bloomers, high-level mature producers, and the successfully aging is that only recently have there been a large number of such adults present in our society. It was reasonable that many decades ago psychologists established longitudinal studies on children to learn in detail how children develop physically, mentally, and socially. This was in response to the social needs for knowledge in an earlier era. Also, the period of development in life is short relative to the life of investigators, so they can make reasonable contributions to their careers and to science by studies of fetal, infant, or child development.

AGE AND WORK

Convincing data demonstrate that humans are living longer, but working shorter. In 1900 the average life expectancy for men and women was 47.3 years (U.S. Department of Health and Human Services, 1987). Today it is 74.7 years. Siegel and Taeuber (1986) have pointed out that the number of persons 65 and over has more than doubled since 1950, reaching 28 million in 1984, while the number of those over the age of 85 has more than quadrupled in the same period. This circumstance of an aging society is brought about by a drop in birthrate, changes in migration, and improved life expectancy. These facts sharpen our interest in the measurement and utilization of the competence and productivity of mature adults.

In spite of the increase in our older population, trends are occurring in our society that result in the massive potential for productivity in the later years remaining untapped. An excellent volume, *Our Aging Society*, edited by Pifer and Bronte (1986), documents the impact of these trends on almost all institutions of our society. For example, as young people have entered the labor force at high school age or college age, there has been pressure for jobs for young adults. One way of relieving this pressure has been to encourage earlier retirement of older workers. Earlier retirement has been sweetened for early retirees by buy-out plans in various industries. Although such policies may represent a short-term solution to resolve the economic problems of companies, they have little to offer regarding the utilization of the potential productivity of older adults for the well-being of society.

Perlmutter (1988a) has suggested that the agenda for research on cognition direct its attention to two major questions: "What are the ways that cognition changes with age?" and "What are the causes of cognitive changes that are associated with age?" She points out in a review of the literature that research has almost always been carried out on a relatively narrow age range and that a broader, that is, a life span, perspective is called for. Individuals are coming from some place (history), are living in a present context, and are going somewhere (older adulthood). In taking a life span perspective, one realizes more fully how effects can accumulate over a longer period of time, and that while they are associated with age, they need not be an inherent consequence of growing older, that is, aging.

Studies of mortality and morbidity in relation to occupational class have shown that, over the employed years, age is much less important than our occupations in determining when we die and from what diseases (Marmot, Shipley, & Rose, 1984). This forces us to take an ecological approach to the life span. If our lengths of life and causes of death are so importantly influenced by occupation, how much more so may be our skills and mental capacities (Birren, 1989). Perlmutter proposes to examine effects of specific work experience and age on occupational performance since the human cognitive system appears to be extremely context dependent and responsive to the specific demands made upon it.

Research on naturally occurring behavior is particularly important for understanding intelligence and the performance of older adults. Experientially based knowledge is central to effective and efficient performance with age. During adult life, individuals gain experience and modify the way subsequent tasks are performed. Yet, we lack a comprehensive understanding of the relationships of work performance and age. Clearly, we need to measure the performance of mature adults in the natural contexts of daily-life occupations. To do this, the development of multiple indices of performance of general and specific skills is required. So is the cooperation of industry and work forces, since suspicions may exist that measurement must either be promanagement or prolabor in its intent, rather than prohuman development. The blend of particular skills required in occupations varies but usually represents a combination of motor, cognitive, and social skills. A recurring theme, though not well demonstrated, has been that the older worker develops organizational strategies that allow work to be performed more effectively, smoothly, and efficiently in the face of concurrent physical and physiological limitations. Thus it is important in our future research to be cautious about generalizing the potentials of older workers from physical assessments of speed, strength, and endurance, or from assessments of organ system capacities to human performance of complex tasks with advancing age.

It seems almost redundant to point out that the development of high-level skills with advancing age requires society to value high-quality performance and encourage its utilization.

LONGITUDINAL STUDIES

We have to develop a knowledge base about the potentials of our mature and elderly population and how best to access these potentials. To meet our obligations to society, we must begin to make plans for establishing major longitudinal studies in significant areas of age and human capacities and productivity. To carry out such studies requires the development of psychological measurements in several neglected areas. For example, we are much more expert at measuring the disorganization of intellectual processes in dementing diseases (Filskov & Boll, 1981) than we are at measuring the abilities that enter into wisdom and divergent thinking and creativity (Alpaugh & Birren, 1975; Clayton, 1975). To meet our current priorities, we must become equally expert on the facts of aging as well as of child development, and on the dynamics of growth and adverse effects on all life stages. One might argue that these are opposite faces of the same coin, that understanding child development and dependency provides a generic understanding of successful old age, but that has not proven to be so. The strengths and vulnerabilities of the phases of life have to be looked at in terms of their own demands.

Most likely, there are many relationships that are not continuous within the human biobehavioral organism. For example, while the deficiency of a vitamin may be related to the quality of performance at the low end, at some point above a deficiency level, that vitamin may cease to be a relevant variable; some vitamin may be vital but more is not necessarily better. In the same way, low income is closely related to life satisfaction, and improvements in life satisfaction may be expected to be related to improvements in income. However, above a mid-level of income the relationship weakens, and no further gains in life satisfaction may be expected to result from increments in income. Like the vitamin example, here some is good, but more is not necessarily better. Health variables may operate in similar ways: After an adequate level of health is reached, further improvements in health status may not be related to increments in life satisfaction and high-level accomplishment. Thus, Olympian health is not likely to be a prerequisite for living a good life in the middle and later years. How much physical activity older adults should engage in is not known. As in vitamins, some is good, but more is not necessarily better.

This suggests that there are boundary conditions on relationships and that nonlinear relationships are typical in many of the domains of human functioning. Matters of health, income, housing, and availability of other persons are prerequisite conditions, but not the necessary and sufficient conditions for determining high-level productivity and creativity. Our measurements have to become specific enough so that we can determine ranges within which influences determine effective human behavior.

COMPONENTS OF ABILITY

Horn's model of the intellect poses that there are two or more major components to intellectual ability. One of these relates to the organized store of long-term information which has been called crystallized ability (Horn & Donaldson, 1980). As mentioned earlier, this component increases with age. It is also responsive to the effects of the environment as demonstrated in the finding that successive cohorts have been higher in crystallized ability. At the same time, measures of intellect that reflect perception and spatial ability may decline with age. In this decline, the role of speed of behavior must be considered. Thus, along with a greater storage of long-term information, there is a slower scanning of information in the long-term store. This may be a reflection of the commonly observed phenomenon that we may know something but not recall it until later. The fact that we do recall the item later indicates that it was not lost, but that it was simply unavailable in retrieval at the right moment. This has been called *benign forgetfulness*, the inability to recall something when it is relevant or when we want it. One of the questions raised has been whether physical fitness plays a role in such forgetfulness. Older individuals who have remained physically fit appear to have faster behavior that includes reaction time and other manifestations. Indeed, older persons who are physically fit and exercise do show quicker reaction times (Woods, 1981). Thus, even a component of intellectual ability that shows a decline, for example, speed of behavior, is possibly reflecting some part of disuse encouraged by culture and the social roles of older persons.

A longitudinal study of Eskimos in Canada who moved from their hunting and gathering area into the city demonstrated a rise in some of the characteristics commonly associated with advancing age, that is, increased body fat, increased blood pressure, and bone demineralization (Sheppard, 1984). Thus, age-linked attributes may not be a consequence of an inherent or a normal species pattern of aging but, rather, a consequence of the environments in which we find ourselves. For this reason, we may now have to exercise in our urban environments to replace the physical load that has been removed by energy-saving devices. As we use less energy in the workplace, we have to spend time and effort in exercise to maintain bodily function in an optimum state. Previously, this was thought only to relate to matters of physical well-being, but it now appears to be related to psychological performance as well. Thus, while some aspects of slowness in retrieval of information may be a norm for the species, it now appears that much of it is a reflection of a sedentary way of life and that change is secondary to age-associated disease.

Adaptive behavioral capacities, such as perception, memory, learning, and creativity, must to some extent be a function of biological involution. However, it is only at the extremes of poor health that one finds a close dependence of psychological capacity on biological processes. It is likely that in reasonably healthy adults there is only a loose coupling between health and behavioral capacities. As yet, we do not have enough information to determine the relative contributions of disease, physical fitness, disuse, and life-long habits. The present state of the research literature leaves us with the impression that selected older adults can sustain a high arousal level in the nervous system and show performance comparable with that of young subjects. Less clear is whether age differences in performance result from a change in the primary information-transmitting system of the brain or are a consequence of alterations in a modulating system, such as that having to do with arousal.

It should be pointed out that the brain is the primary integrative system of the body. It is responsible not only for the integrity of our behavior, but also for our capacity to adapt to environmental changes of temperature and the demands for effort. The brain regulates both the vegetative systems necessary for survival as well as the components of behavior that give value to life for us as human beings. More often studied in psychological research have been the components of ability rather than the orchestration of abilities in complex performance and the role of capacities that may be identified in terms of wisdom and divergent thinking.

THE MEASUREMENT OF ABILITY

Much of the effort in psychological research has been devoted to the development of measures of abilities. These abilities permit humans to represent and think about the world, conceptualize experience, fantasize beyond experience and be creative, maintain a sense of self, and communicate with others. They include perception, memory, intelligence, reasoning, judgment, and decision-making. They allow us to solve and circumvent problems, give us power to anticipate and plan for the future, and enable us to profit from a wide range of experiences.

However, the fact that we have many abilities does not necessarily imply that we use them. Lack of use of abilities in the schoolroom may lead to the characterization of a child as being retarded. In a similar way, older adults can be depreciated as having lost abilities if they are not observed to demonstrate them. Lack of opportunity to show cognitive skills may be an important factor. Perlmutter (1988b) has suggested that we have been much too prone to assume a universal decline in adult intellectual abilities without looking at the effects of the context of daily life and occupational requirements.

We should expect that future psychological research about mature adults will include observations in the third and fourth quarter of life and will provide data not only on what people do with their time and how they use their performance potentials, but also on how circumstances of the environment mediate these tendencies. Lack of opportunities in the environment of older adults may lead to the neglect of many specialized abilities, including those that are used in graphic arts, music, linguistic skills, and dance.

One of the dominant topics in psychological research is the study of the development and aging of intellectual abilities. While this research is not yet complete in terms of separating the contributions of cohort differences in education, health, and other factors, it appears that the nervous system continues to gain information throughout the course of life. It has no upper limit. In fact, when one begins to lose information, it is most commonly due to an erosion of health (Birren, Butler, Greenhouse, Sokoloff, & Yarrow, 1963). Thus, we do not "top off" at a particular age, but continue to gain information that is put into our long-term storage. When measures of information show an older adult as undergoing losses, one should be suspicious of concurrent disease. Such changes are often linked to a period called *terminal decline* in which approaching death may involve a constellation of changes that are qualitatively different from previous competencies and the manner of life of the individual.

Increasing attention must be given to those measures of intellectual performance and ability that reflect or are sensitive to illness and terminal decline. In this way, measurements of behavior can be used to develop a sensitive index to alterations in the physiology of the aging organism that may not be expressed early as frank disease. Here, the point is that the output of our complex nervous system in the form of behavior may be used as a sensitive indicator of physiological bodily change during the employed years as well as in retirement. In this regard, more longitudinal measurements of behavior are required.

It is quite reasonable that the more complex the process, the more likely it is to reveal subtle changes in components. Handwriting, for example, can reveal health changes. One of us was told that a signature by President Franklin Roosevelt early on the morning of his death had so changed that it would not have been taken as a legal signature. In this case, President Roosevelt died of a stroke that was forewarned by a change in the complex behavior of handwriting. Related to this is the use of behavioral and neuropsychological measurements associated with the measurement of drug and alcohol effects.

THE MEASUREMENT OF
HUMAN BEHAVIOR

It is timely that behavioral scientists turn to the measurement of human behavior in a more comprehensive sense than they have in the past. We have been greatly influenced by the need to study performance in specific behaviors. During the school years we examine in great detail the learning and performance of such skills as arithmetic, spelling, English, or history. On the playground we measure specific athletic skills. However, these studies measure behaviors in isolation; rarely do we conceive of human behavior as forming a unity characterizing the individual.

An early experiment that attempted such unity was initiated by several psychologists following a child through a 24-hour period (Barker & Wright, 1954). In this manner a record was made of all the transactions in which the child engaged during the day. Later, this experiment was extended to the tracking of older persons in Midwest America and comparing them to a community in England. Such comparisons are vital to our understanding of how behavior is organized.

Research on different distributions of activities by time, age, sex, economic class, and other categories is important for our understanding of the development of our aging population. For example, the amount of time spent by adults of different ages in information exchange is significant. On the one hand, we can measure the exposure to information through time spent in reading books, newspapers, and magazines; viewing television; or speaking to other persons. This represents a pattern of information gain from the environment. We do not have much information about the quality and quantity of information in the stream of daily life, or the resources in the sphere of daily life activities. On the other hand, we can measure the provision of information to the environment by an individual by documenting the amount of time spent in initiating and conducting information exchange in telephone conversations or writing letters.

In the latter approach, productivity can be defined by the exchange of information and energy from an individual. Some of our most productive activities are the result of the generation of novel solutions to problems, solutions that often reduce the need for monetized exchanges. It is here where a psychological view of human productivity differs from the economist's view. Examination of individual differences in the distribution of activities over time will give us hints about the ways in which the utilization of the productive potentials of older persons can be maximized.

Measurements of the varieties of the uses of time and the distribution of time, information, and activities by individuals of various ages also establish baselines. It is expected that a major effort to study these distributions of time in adult life will produce new theories about aging and human productivity. In addition, it will lead to clues about developing environments that can utilize the productivity of older persons in ways that will enhance their fulfillment as well as the attainment of a meaningful life and good mental health.

THE MEASUREMENT OF PRODUCTIVITY

The economic return of a worker's effort is easily expressed in terms of dollars. But perhaps we have been lulled into defining productivity solely in terms of money. It is about time that we consider alternative concepts of productivity and devote attention to their measurement. The task is to define the productivity of men and women across the life span in such a way that it more adequately reflects their contributions to society and leads to the identification of untapped potential.

The present authors would like to illustrate the issue of age and productivity with two examples. One of us, in the last three years, has had the experience of adding a room to a house in order to house the books, papers, and writing equipment of an active professional life. The contractor who added the room was over the age of 65. He had been a resident in the community for 40 years and had one carpenter working with him for 30 years and another for 20 years. At the completion of the addition, with all of its cabinetry and special requirements, there was not a single complaint or callback on any of the construction or installation. The combined experience of the workers was such that no modifications in their work were necessary. This is not unlike the situation with our second example, automobiles, which may be produced by two systems of quality control. In one system you expect to have the dealer fix or modify features of the automobile that left the factory in an inadequate condition. The other approach is to have high-quality control in the factory prior to shipment; here, one does not budget the dealer for a cleanup operation. This second pattern also results in savings of time by the purchaser. In the same sense, the author who added the library was free of not only the expense of time necessary to recall the contractor, but also the monetary expense. The experience of the workers ensured initial quality. Today at age 70, the contractor only takes occasional jobs, the ones he deems interesting.

Any jobs he does take, however, show a level of competence and contribution that goes beyond the actual cost of his time and effort. Thus, productivity is not measured in its fullest sense by the original exchange of dollars between workers and their employer.

Another aspect of productivity that is difficult to measure lies in the mental health area. Today's society requires that both husbands and wives work, and so children are raised in a busy and often strident household as people rush to meet their obligations. Little opportunity is provided for the children to absorb the guidance drawn from full parental attention. Often, a grandparent provides the stabilizing attitudes and points of view that give the psychological life of the child its solidity and character to meet demands over a long life.

Another feature of our aging society is that as we live longer, there are more generations alive at one time in extended families than ever before. It is not unusual now to find five generations alive in a single family. At the same time, there is increasing divorce, so within the longer extended family there are more broken relations and disrupted responsibilities for child rearing. Into this pattern often fit roles for the grandparents in dealing with the psychological development of the child. A harried mother finds it more difficult to deal with the needs of a hyperkinetic child than a grandparent who is feeling less pressure from the calls of the marketplace. The grandparent can indeed become the psychological anchor for the child's life. We often find that students today who are entering the field of gerontology and related professions have had an excellent relationship with a grandfather or grandmother. They feel positively about the elderly, and they often verbalize a desire to return something of what they received.

Mentoring in the workplace by the mature adult is also an asset, both to the employer and to the maturing worker. This is similar to the asset in the university where the mentoring role of faculty to students is well established. Mentoring involves not only the guidance of skill acquisition but also the contributions of task approach strategies and self-management that are possessed by model seniors.

Another area of contribution can be the disabled child, who is often a handicap for the busy adult parent. Often a grandparent can give the unrestricted love and attention to the child that is problematic or conflicted for the parent. How does one measure the productivity of a grandparent in strengthening the mental health of a child? In our concept, this is a capital investment in the future, an investment parallel to that of the school system in knowledge development. The payoff is many years later when the competent and mentally strong child becomes a leader and productive adult, or the handicapped child has maximized his or her potential and is a contributing member in the social system.

The book *Our Aging Society* (Pifer & Bronte, 1986) uses the concept of the third quarter of life in referring to the age range of 50 to 75 as that in which most persons retire. Today, about 50 million people are in the third quarter, and by the year 2010 it is expected that there will be 85 million persons in the third quarter. Pifer points out that most people over age 50 today "are vigorous, in good health, mentally alert, and capable of making a productive contribution until they are at least 75" (1986, p. 402). The point here, however, is that potentials for productivity go well into the years beyond 75. It is only when we focus on the issue of monetized exchanges that we take a constricted view of productivity. We have not yet given proper attention to contributions in which there are no dollar exchanges, such as those to the mental health of families that are made by people in their 80s and 90s.

WISDOM AND DIVERGENT THINKING

In addition to maintaining and increasing one's store of long-term information and executing complex behavior, such as handwriting, operating a word processor, or driving an automobile, there is the issue of generating new ideas. Lower organisms adapt to their environments primarily by the use of behaviors that the species' evolution has provided. Humans, however, adapt through the modification of the nervous system as a result of experience. A good portion of the programming of the central nervous system arises from experience.

In addition to the behaviors that are provided by the genome, and those provided by experience, there is also the generation of novel behaviors through creativity or divergent thinking. The use of stored knowledge and performance on components of intellectual ability does not necessarily predict creativity. Thus, apart from intelligence itself, there may be a change with age in the preference for complexity and the desire to exercise creativity (Alpaugh & Birren, 1975). There may be two different components of creativity: one, a set of abilities that can be readily measured, and another that is more difficult to measure, that of the motivational component of creativity. The desire to generate a novel solution to a problem appears to be not wholly a matter of the ability to do it. Expectations of our social environments, as well as our own personalities, will dictate the extent to which we will try a novel solution to an old task, let alone a new circumstance. Risk taking in generating novel or divergent thought can be suppressed in older adults much as it is in restrictive classroom atmospheres of the school years.

The tendency for divergent thinking may be discouraged with advancing age and may fall into disuse (McCrae, 1987; McCrae, Arenberg, & Costa, 1987). There is evidence that the generation of novel ideas, hypotheses, and playful manipulations of perceptions is lower in older adults than it is in the young. Some older adults retain a playfulness of mind that leads to the generation of new ideas. However, apparently there is a tendency with age to rely on redundancy of previously used solutions. In the classroom, the young child with a divergent trend of mind creates disturbances. As a result, the frustrated teacher may repress the tendency to divergent thinking. In a similar way, divergent thinking in an older adult may be problematic in a social context since it may place a transient information overload on others. Nevertheless, the generation of novel solutions is a requirement for adaptive human behavior. Evolution has given us a nervous system that is programmed on the basis of experience; and the manipulation of long-term store in relation to environmental demands dictates that we generate new strategies.

It has been suggested that wisdom is one of the qualities in the later years that enhances the value of the older adult. Wisdom has been viewed as a complex trait consisting of a large amount of relevant experience, a capacity to reason, familiarity with cultural context, and the motivation to come up with new solutions. Here is an area that calls for new measurements and concepts. It would seem that the tendency to divergent thinking has to be encouraged if the older adult is to be wise and to serve not only him or herself but also the family and community. Certainly, living through the issues of growing up; establishing a family; enduring the consequences of depressions, wars, and financial reversals; and assuming complex adult responsibilities should equip the older adult to perform an unusual service. In this context, a degree of emotional detachment may also enhance the "wisdom" of the mature adult. Older adults appear to derive a higher level of satisfaction from their material and social circumstances than do young adults (Butt & Beiser, 1987).

It is commonly thought that unlike the young, older adults are less interested in "What is in it for them." They can respond more to the needs of the other, whether it be a child, an adult, or a circumstance of society. The capacity to be somewhat emotionally distant while still vitally alive to the demands of a current circumstance would provoke wisdom. It is hard to attribute wisdom to young adults given their tendency to impulsive acts. Reflection and detachment provide the intellectual context for weighing and generating alternatives. Wisdom does not appear to be built solely by component abilities, but is also seasoned by the emotion and affect.

Tests of divergent thinking have shown that results are lower if measured after the subject takes convergent tests where the focus is on one and only one correct answer to a question. Thus, it appears that divergent thinking is affected by the environmental context and the state of the organism or its outlook at the time of testing. Similarly, creativity has been linked to emotional or affective components of life. In a society that devalues the status of the older adult, that is, where older adults are viewed as declining in productivity and ability, motivation to show divergent thinking and engage in creative acts is reasonably diminished.

Preliminary studies will have to be made on individuals who have demonstrated high creativity and wisdom in their later years, in contrast to those who have shown constricted capacity and involution.

SUMMARY

Over the decades that aging has been considered by academics and researchers, the topic of successful aging often has been addressed. The difficulty in this concept rests on the fact that there are so many different perspectives about successful aging. Successful aging looks different from the point of view of a physician, a biologist, a psychologist, and a social scientist. These perspectives may, in turn, differ from the point of view of the individual who has lived his or her life and has a different sense about what makes for success. Rather than projecting a single criterion of successful aging, perhaps some of the components might be investigated. Among those at the biological level that contribute to psychological well-being are the concepts of longevity and vigor. One of the basic questions is the extent to which a full and productive life is supported by the individual whose familial background has provided a high level of vigor and the potentials for longevity. Technically, it raises the question of the extent to which these biological predispositions of vigor and longevity are co-varying with psychological capacities of competency, productivity, creativity, and intellectual abilities.

Given our current levels of skill in generating complex research designs, it is now time to promote research that examines pathways to well-being in the fullest sense of the social, psychological, and physical well-being of mature and elderly persons. Earlier in the century when cross-sectional and longitudinal studies were planned on child development, they were necessarily limited not only by the concepts of the day but also by methods of statistical analysis and computer capacity. Advances of scientific methods have equipped us as never before to plan and conduct studies that will enhance our potentials for well-being in the later years. It is clearly time that research be planned and supported to address questions about well-being throughout the course of human life. We should think about this in relation to adequate samples for study. Past studies, for the most part, have been characterized by opportunistic samples in limited geographic regions and by limited social class backgrounds of the subjects.

Along with the measurement of human capacities we must explore the compensations for deficits in human capacities. Many of our current measurements do not lend themselves to detecting reserve capacity or the compensations the individual may use to obviate limits or deficits, or to maintain or expand competence. For these purposes, research should examine matters of competency in the natural contexts of daily life rather than only in the laboratory. Aging is a result of ecological relationships, and the omission of the context of daily life from the assessment of competency is a severe limitation on our ability to generalize from lab to life.

No scientific question has greater scope and significance than that of why living systems age, with attendant implications for health and well-being of humankind and the quality of life of older adults in contemporary society. The inadequacy of scientific knowledge about aging is limiting our ability to be productive and function independently. Asserting a national goal of improving the mental and physical health of the older population reflects the public's restlessness for improvement in a wide range of practical matters that bear on the quality of life, such as health care systems and their costs, housing, pension plans, opportunities for work and learning, and care of the terminally ill elderly. Progress in these matters requires research. This research will not only make possible the improvement of specific problems of the elderly, but also obviate many of the costs of current programs through effective health promotion. If an optimum environment is to be developed so individuals can realize their full biological and psychological potentials not only in youth and middle age but in late life as well, we must have facts based upon research. We must improve our fundamental understanding of the processes of aging on which future services and sound administration of programs can be based. Without such fundamental understanding, we will fail to make substantial progress in enhancing the quality of life.

Research on aging is a vast scientific frontier with prospects for gains in many aspects of humankind's well-being. As we approach the end of the 20th century, there is a new context for research on aging that is in several important ways different from that surrounding the pioneers who initiated gerontological research earlier in this century. The growth of the number and proportion of older persons has created what some have called the demographic imperative, an imperative that forces changes in almost every institution of our society. Hospitals, institutions of higher learning, business, and religious institutions all must adapt to the older society. The enormity of the demographic shift is revealed by the fact that the United States has more persons over the age of 65 than the total population of Canada. There are few countries in Europe that have total populations larger than just our population over the age of 65. We have a growing "nation" of better educated older persons with higher expectations that must be met, and this must help to set our research agendas.

REFERENCES

Alpaugh, P. K., & Birren, J. E. (1975). Are there sex differences in creativity across the adult life span? *Human Development, 18,* 461–465.

Alpaugh, P. K., Renner, V. J., & Birren, J. E. (1976). Age and creativity: Implications for education and teachers. *Journal of Educational Gerontology, 1,* 17–40.

Barker, R. G., & Wright, H. F. (1954). *Midwest and its children.* Evanston, Ill.: Row, Peterson.

Birren, J. E. (1989). A contribution to theory of the psychology of aging: As a counterpart of development. In J. E. Birren & V. L. Bengtson (Eds.), *Emergent theories of aging.* New York: Springer Publishing Co.

Birren, J. E., Butler, R. N., Greenhouse, S. W., Sokoloff, L., & Yarrow, M. (Eds.). (1963). *Human aging.* Washington, DC: U.S. Government Printing Office.

Butt, S. D., & Beiser, M. (1987). Successful aging: A theme for international psychology. *Psychology and Aging, 2*, 87–94.

Clayton, V. (1975). A multidimensional scaling analysis of the concept of wisdom. Unpublished doctoral dissertation (Psychology), University of Southern California, Los Angeles.

Cunningham, W. R., & Birren, J. E. (1976). Age changes in human abilities: A 28-year longitudinal study. *Develop. Psychology, 12*, 81–82.

Filskov, S. B., & Boll, T. J. (Eds.). (1981). *Handbook of clinical neuropsychology.* New York: Wiley.

Horn, J. L., & Donaldson, G. (1980). Cognitive development in adulthood. In O. G. Brim & J. Kagan (Eds.), *Constancy and change in human development* (pp. 445–529). Cambridge, MA: Harvard University Press.

Labouvie-Vief, G. (1985). Intelligence and cognition. In J. E. Birren & K. W. Schaie (Eds.), *Handbook of the psychology of aging* (pp. 500–529). New York: Van Nostrand Reinhold.

Marmot, M. G., Shipley, M. J., & Rose, G. (1984). Inequalities in death-specific explanations of a general pattern? *Lancet*, 1003–1006.

McCrae, R. R. (1987). Creativity, divergent thinking, and openness to experience. *J. Person. & Soc. Psychol., 52*, 1258–1265.

McCrae, R. R., Arenberg, D., & Costa, P. T. (1987). Declines in divergent thinking with age: Cross-sectional, longitudinal, and cross-sequential analysis. *Psychology & Aging, 2*, 130–137.

Perlmutter, M. (1988a). Cognitive development in life span perspective: From description of differences to explanation of changes. In M. Hetherington, R. Lerner, & M. Perlmutter (Eds.), *Child development in life span perspective.* Hillside, N.J.: Erlbaum Associates.

Perlmutter, M. (1988b). Cognitive potential throughout life. In J. E. Birren & V. L. Bengtson (Eds.), *Emergent theories in aging.* Hillside, N.J.: Erlbaum Associates.

Pifer, A. (1986). The public policy response. In A. Pifer & Bronte, L. (Eds.), *Our aging society* (pp. 391–413). New York: Norton.

Pifer, A., & Bronte, L. (Eds.). (1986). *Our aging society.* New York: Norton.

Seashore, R. H., & Eckerson, L. D. (1940). The measurement of individual differences in general English vocabularies. *J. Ed. Psychol., 31*, 14–29.

Sheppard, R. J. (1984). Technological change and the aging of working capacity. In P. K. Robinson, J. Livingston, & J. E. Birren

(Eds.), *Aging and technological advances* (pp. 195–207). New York: Plenum.

Siegel, J. S., & Taeuber, C. M. (1986). Demographic dimensions of an aging society. In A. Pifer & L. Bronte (Eds.), *Our aging society* (pp. 79–110). New York: Norton.

U.S. Department of Health and Human Services. (1984). Vital Statistics of the United States. 1984. Life Table, Volume II, Section 6 (DHHS Publication No. PHS 87-1104). Washington, DC: U.S. Government Printing Office.

Woods, A. M. (1981). Age differences in the effect of physical activity and postural changes on information processing. Unpublished doctoral dissertation (Psychology), University of Southern California, Los Angeles.

The Brain: New Plasticity/ New Possibility

6

Carl W. Cotman

INTRODUCTION

Productive aging requires a productive brain. It is widely believed that the brain shows progressive functional decline with age and has little or no regenerative capacity. Yet many persons lead full productive lives in their later years. With age, neurons die and the brain falls increasingly vulnerable to small strokes and age-related neurodegenerative diseases. As the most sophisticated of all tissues, it would certainly be expected that the brain would possess at least a limited capacity to repair age-related losses and those due to minor injuries to its intricate circuitries. Other tissues (skin, liver, muscle, etc.) have mechanisms to repair damage. Unlike most tissues, however, brain cells do not divide after a person is born. A person has the vast majority of their brain cells at birth and they are not naturally replaced. Does the brain have a program to maintain, adapt, and repair itself from neuron loss and dysfunction, and if so, what is it?

Recent neuroscience research on the structure and function of brain cells suggests that functional loss is not an inevitable consequence of aging. The brain has an inherent plastic capacity to compensate for functional deficits and even for minor loss of its neurons. Here, recent findings on the capacity of the brain to regenerate new connections, maintain function, and even heal itself will be discussed. A better understanding of the brain's processes might help to increase the number of people who experience productive aging.

NEURONS, BRAIN NETWORKS, AND LOSS WITH AGE

The number, design, and connections of the brain's neurons determine to a large measure the capacity of the total brain. Neurons are the fundamental genetic, anatomical, functional, and trophic (nutritive or sustaining) units of the nervous system. These brain cells are large or small, simple or complex, according to their tasks. Neurons have many processes extending from the cell body. Each neuron has a fine process (an axon) that extends from the cell body to other neurons where it makes connections (synapses) with them. These synapses empower the brain with its computational ability. Each one is a nodal point of functional activity that processes transient events and stores key ones long term. The maintenance and plastic capabilities of synapses are essential for the aged brain.

Neurons are organized in elaborate networks, like miniaturized circuits in a computer. Redundancy and parallel processing are two of the key organizing principles of the brain. Neurons work in units, in teams, often with many members seemingly alike, carrying out the same transactions and forming connections in parallel with their partners. This increases the reliability of the network and its computational capacity, and makes it more resistant to the loss of one or more of the members of the team. Minor losses are compensated for by others assuming responsibility. Of course, even with redundancy and parallel processing, losses will eventually translate into poorer function if too many neurons die and their loss is not compensated.

With age, some neurons die due to age itself, increased susceptibility to pathology, and an accumulation of environmental insults. There are several noticeable gross changes in the aged human brain, such as a decline in brain volume and weight, enlargement of the ventricles, and narrowing of the gyri and sulci. For several decades it was believed that the loss of neurons was quite major, leading the brain to follow a continual and irreversible downhill course.

Recently, it has been shown that neuron loss in the healthy aged brain is much less severe than previously believed. Neuron loss is not an inevitable consequence of aging, although it can occur. Surprisingly, the total number of neurons, neuronal density, and percentage of cell area in the cerebral cortex changes little, if any, with normal aging (Terry, DeTeresa, & Hansen, 1987). The number of large neurons appears to decline (Fig. 6.1*A*), but the number of small neurons shows a consequent increase (Fig. 6.1*B*). After 55 years of age, for example, there is a progressive increase in the number of small neurons, although there is wide variation within the population. This increase in small neurons appears to be due to the atrophy of large neurons, since the total number of cells does not change significantly.

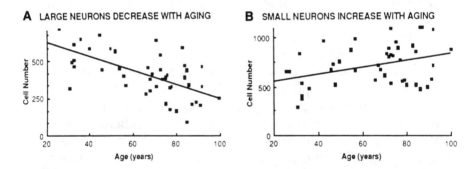

Figure 6.1. Aging leads to alterations in neuronal and glial cell populations. Brains from a group of 51 individuals with normal cognitive function were used in this study. The brains were fixed and sectioned at 20 microns. After staining with cresyl violet, cortical cells were counted with a quantimet 920 (data redrawn from Terry et al., 1987). (*A*) Large neurons (> 90 microns) show a strong negative correlation with aging in all the midfrontal, superior temporal, and inferior parietal areas of the neocortex. (*B*) Small neurons (< 90 microns but > 40 microns) increase in number with advancing age.

Apparently, several of the early reports on neuron changes with age included brain tissues from persons with diseases and failed to recognize that some of the larger neurons had shrunk rather than died.

Small neurons would be expected to have less integrative capacity than large ones since they have fewer synapses and can handle less information. The reason neurons become smaller is unknown. Large neurons may shrink due to a lack of adequate trophic influences, minor disuse, or other unknown causes. In some brain areas neurons do degenerate with age. This occurs particularly in those areas most susceptible to pathologies and age-related degenerative diseases (see Cotman & Peterson, 1987, for discussion).

REMAINING NEURONS REPLACE
OLD SYNAPSES WITH NEW

The brain has been classically viewed as being "hard-wired." The basic plan is laid down during development and changes little with age except for losses such as those due to neuronal pathology or death. It is now clear, however, that with neuron loss the healthy neurons react by growing and replacing the lost synapses.

When a fraction of an input to a neuron or group of neurons is lost (the X in Fig. 6.2A), the nerve fibers from undamaged neurons often sprout and form new connections in place of those lost (the arrows in Fig. 6.2A). This phenomenon, called *axon sprouting*, was first clearly identified in the 1950s in the peripheral nervous system. When a few motor fibers were cut, those remaining sprouted new side branches and made new synapses with the muscle (Edds, 1953; Hoffman, 1950). In this way the remaining fibers are able to assume the function of those lost. Subsequently this process was observed in the autonomic nervous system, spinal cord, and brain. It is now apparent that such synaptic regrowth and replacement is widespread, occurring in both the peripheral and central nervous systems (for review, see Cotman, Nieto-Sampedro, & Harris, 1981).

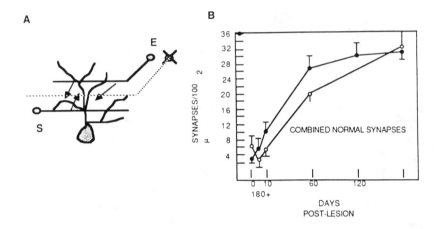

Figure 6.2. Axon sprouting and reactive synapse formation. (*A*) When neurons degenerate (thin dashed line), the remaining neurons sprout (arrows) and make new synapses to replace the lost ones. E, entorhinal neurons; S, septal neurons. (*B*) The course for the replacement of new synapses in the rodent brain after an entorhinal lesion (data from Hoff et al., 1982). Solid circles = mature adult; open circles = aged.

The basic phenomenon and its robustness can be illustrated by considering the consequence of damage to part of the rodent cerebral cortex called the entorhinal cortex. Loss of neurons in this area causes the loss of over 50% of the synapses in its target, the hippocampus. This loss, however, is transient, and over a period of a few weeks synapses are replaced (Fig. 6.2B). The remaining cells that connect to neurons that have lost a portion of their input sprout and make new functional synapses (for review, see Cotman & Nieto-Sampedro, 1984; Nieto-Sampedro & Cotman, 1985). Synapse replacement, however, is virtually complete in both the aged and the mature brain (Hoff, Scheff, Benardo, & Cotman, 1982), though the rate of initiation of growth is slower in the aged brain. This regenerative process is important in this particular example, since entorhinal neurons appear to die in old age and are particularly vulnerable to Alzheimer's disease (Hyman, Van Hoesen, Damasio, & Barnes, 1984).

AXON SPROUTING

Research on animal models then predicts that axon sprouting might occur in the aged human brain and the brain of patients with Alzheimer's disease. Alzheimer's disease is an irreversible degenerative disease associated with pathology and a slow loss of neurons. This disease is accompanied by a selective loss of neurons in the entorhinal cortex. In rodents, loss of these neurons triggers growth of select inputs to the target cells in the hippocampus including its input, which uses acetylcholine as its neurotransmitter (Cotman & Nieto-Sampedro, 1984). These nerve fibers sprout in the area where entorhinal fibers have degenerated.

Is the slow degeneration of neurons in Alzheimer's disease accompanied by a growth process similar to that seen in rodents that rebuilds lost connections? In many cases of Alzheimer's disease there is often a selective and profound loss of neurons that use the transmitter acetylcholine. However, neuronal loss in the entorhinal cortex can also occur in patients without a corresponding loss of acetylcholine-using neurons.

In patients where acetylcholine-using neurons are present, their fibers sprout in the synaptic field where entorhinal input declines (Geddes et al., 1985; Fig. 6.3). Thus, these acetylcholine-using neurons are capable of sprouting in humans in the course of this disease. This reaction is qualitatively similar to that previously described in the rodent brain after entorhinal lesions. It appears that the neuronal loss in the entorhinal cortex of Alzheimer's disease patients acts as a stimulus in a manner similar to that of a lesion in the rat brain. These sprouted fibers appear to augment remaining excitatory cortical input (see Cotman & Anderson, 1988, for discussion). Compensatory growth in the course of a degenerative disease indicates that the resultant circuitry does not merely reflect a loss of neural elements.

Thus, as the cells are lost, new connections made by the healthy cells from within the population can assume parallel functions or the fibers from converging pathways can, as in the case of the acetylcholine input, boost weakened signals and maintain functional stability in the wake of cell loss (see Cotman

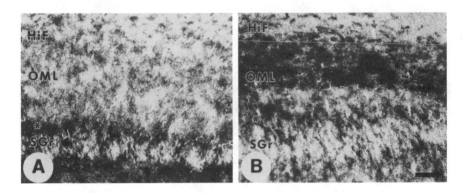

Figure 6.3. Axon sprouting of acetylcholine-using neurons in the hippocampus of patients who died of Alzheimer's disease (AD). The loss of entorhinal neurons in this degenerative disease causes compensatory growth of acetylcholine neurons. This input to the molecular layer (OML) of the dentate gyrus (*A*) in a normal subject shows a diffuse uniform pattern. The input increases in the AD brain (*B*).

& Anderson, 1988). Reactive growth can, in principle, help maintain function if a portion of the relay is still intact. The clinical threshold, where functions may disappear, is at least postponed so that the nervous system can counteract the loss of its circuits. It causes the remaining cells to assume more of the work load but keeps the connections at their normal levels. As the system continues to compensate, however, it may become progressively more unreliable and unstable so that functional decline may be very rapid.

SPROUTING IN THE NORMAL AGED BRAIN

Does sprouting take place in the normal aged brain? Recent work has again focused on the hippocampus, a brain region critical for learning and memory but also very vulnerable to damage in disease. Neurons have giant dendritic arbors that offer vast surfaces on which synapses are formed by other neurons. The shape and luxuriance of the dendritic tree are critical to the total interactive capacity of those cells.

Only a few years ago it was thought that the dendrites atrophy with age, shrinking their arbors and thus reducing the impulse traffic they can handle. On the contrary, the dendritic arbors actually grow between middle and old age (Coleman & Flood, 1986; Fig. 6.4). The fine branches at the tips of the dendrites develop more branches. Only in very old age does the dendritic tree appear to regress but then only compared to that of mature adults. Dendritic growth is particularly prominent in brain areas that show some neuronal loss (or atrophy) with age. The remaining cells fill up the space, responding to emptiness. In some brain areas, these compensation mechanisms may be part of the lifelong program to maintain and adapt brain function. It is survival of the fittest neurons. Neurons look out for themselves, competing for resources, just like the total person they manage. These neurons, the healthy surviving ones, assume functions, as members of the team fall victim to age. In Alzheimer's disease, the extra growth appears less (Coleman & Flood, 1986), but most of these cells are no worse off than those of the mature adult. The brain sustains its elements, its circuits, and in doing so, the person.

GROWTH FACTORS

In the developing, mature, and aged nervous system, neurons depend on a class of molecules called growth factors. Growth factors—specifically, polypeptide growth factors (PGFs)—are proteins that promote the growth and survival of various tissues in the body (James & Bradshaw, 1984). The nervous system has its own specific nerve growth factors but also, curiously, shares growth factors with other nonneural tissues. Nerve growth factors are essential for the survival and growth of the brain's neurons. These molecules appear to be obtained from the target cells of each neuron; the target cells nourish and sustain their input cells. Loss of target cells or cutting of the neuron's axon input during development deprives them of

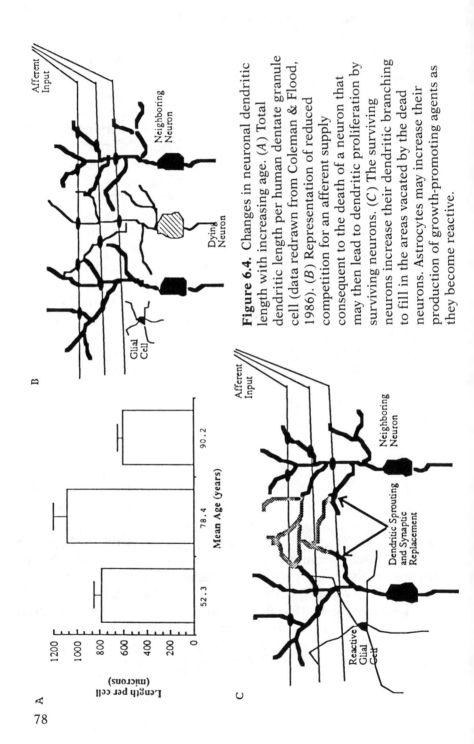

Figure 6.4. Changes in neuronal dendritic length with increasing age. (*A*) Total dendritic length per human dentate granule cell (data redrawn from Coleman & Flood, 1986). (*B*) Representation of reduced competition for an afferent supply consequent to the death of a neuron that may then lead to dendritic proliferation by surviving neurons. (*C*) The surviving neurons increase their dendritic branching to fill in the areas vacated by the dead neurons. Astrocytes may increase their production of growth-promoting agents as they become reactive.

78

their growth factors, causing the cells to become smaller and eventually to degenerate.

It appears that injury to the central nervous system (CNS) causes an increase in the activity of growth factors in injured parts of the CNS (Nieto-Sampedro & Cotman, 1985; Fig. 6.5). The increased amount of these factors may regulate sprouting and help maintain injured neurons. In the developing, mature, or aged rodent brain, injury causes a time-dependent rise in the activity of these factors. After brain injury, extracts of both tissue and fluids around the injury show increased amounts of growth factor activity. In the tissue surrounding the wound, the maximal levels of trophic activity are successively higher in neonatal, adult, and aged animals, and they are reached at 3, 10, and 15 days after injury, respectively. The activity of nerve growth factors is highest near the injured site and decays with distance (Nieto-Sampedro et al., 1983; Needels et al., 1986). These injury-induced factors probably participate in axon and dendritic sprouting, in facilitating transplant survival, and even in saving cells from dying after their axons are cut (for review, see Nieto-Sampedro & Cotman, 1985).

Recently, it has been shown that delivery of an appropriate purified growth factor rescues damaged neurons from dying. If axons of the acetylcholine-using neurons projecting to the

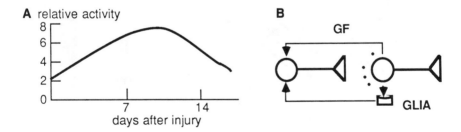

Figure 6.5. Growth factors (GF) and injury-induced growth factors in the brain. (*A*) The activity of specific growth factors increases over the first several days after injury reaching a peak in the first 1 to 2 weeks. (*B*) Growth factors appear to be produced by target neurons (or possibly glia) and are transported back to the cell body where they provide trophic (nutritive) influences to the neurons.

hippocampus are cut, these neurons atrophy and die over a period of one to two weeks. Fibroblast growth factor (FGF), however, prevents their degeneration (Anderson et al., 1988; Fig. 6.6). FGF can even be introduced several hours after injury to prevent neuronal loss, though the number saved declines with time after injury. FGF prevents atrophy and degeneration of neurons in both the adult or aged brain.

These data raise the prospect that nerve growth factors may prove to be an appropriate therapeutic strategy to minimize the effects of traumatic injury and perhaps even neuronal atrophy with age. The increase of growth factors after injury (see above), may act as a natural preventative mechanism to counteract degeneration. An adequate supply of growth factors may help minimize cell loss and pathology. This induction, however, requires several days to develop. Supplying factors earlier appears to improve their effectiveness. Recent data in fact suggests that a particular growth factor (NGF) can improve the functional capacity of the normal aged brain when infused into it (Fischer et al., 1987).

Work on growth factors is significant because it shows that damaged or even atrophied neurons can be rescued by pharma-

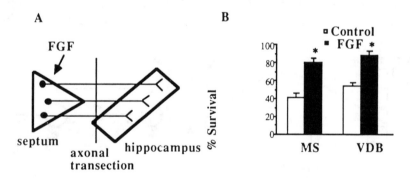

Figure 6.6. Fibroblast growth factor and neuronal survival. (*A*) Cutting fibers from neurons in the septum causes over half of the neurons to degenerate. FGF can prevent degeneration. (*B*) Percent of cholinergic neurons in lesioned relative to unlesioned septum in FGF treated and untreated (control) animals. *$p < 0.025$ (data from Anderson et al., 1988)

cological intervention. Although these factors work within the brain, they are large molecules that are prevented from entering the brain from the outside. Thus, currently, it is not possible to deliver them by oral or intravenous methods. Perhaps in the near future ways to regulate their production or readily deliver them will be discovered. Increasing their production by other drugs or stimuli may help to improve brain function in the elderly.

EFFECT OF TRAINING AND/OR EXPERIENCE ON NEURON STRUCTURE

As illustrated in the previous sections, the brain's neurons are capable of growth and remodeling in response to injury or with natural aging. Many studies have demonstrated that early experience during development can also shape neuronal structure (for review, see Greenough, 1984; Cotman & Lynch, 1987). It is now clear that subtle but significant effects can also be demonstrated in adults. Rats appear to have a paw preference much as people are right or left handed. In one experiment, mature rats were trained to reach for food with their nonpreferred paw (Greenough et al., 1985). Normally the large neurons in the motor cortex on the side of the brain that controls the preferred paw have more elaborate dendrites than those on the opposite side. After 16 days of training, however, dendritic branching increases on the side controlling the newly trained paw. Experience and/or learning thus appears capable of building circuitry in the mature brain. Similar experiments on the aged brain have not been reported to date though the increase in dendrites in the aged human brain may reflect in part a lifetime of experience.

CONCLUSION

The process of aging in the brain is an interaction of age-related losses, disease, and compensatory mechanisms that work to offset functional declines. While most studies emphasize age-related losses, many properties in specific systems are preserved (e.g., neuron number, synaptic transmission in select brain pathways, oxidative cerebral metabolism, etc.; see Cotman & Peterson, 1987, for review). Heterogeneity is one of the hallmarks of aging (see Rowe, this volume). Adaptive or plastic mechanisms probably play a key role in maintaining functions during aging. Aging of the brain probably is due not to a single factor but rather to a series of interdependent mechanisms that ultimately compromise the precision and computational accuracy of its networks.

Reactive sprouting and other plastic mechanisms may offset functional losses with aging. Sprouting also may function in the course of some degenerative disorders. Exogenously supplied growth factors can help neurons and offer a possible means of interventive therapy. Neurons can respond to a favorable environment. Perhaps, by following these plastic processes, it will be possible to develop interventions along these natural lines of defense and further improve CNS function with age. Research along these lines may also provide new clues on the fundamental issue: what leads to cell atrophy and loss in the first place. Reactive regrowth of neural circuitries certainly indicates that the brain can mobilize its resources and that the system is sufficiently vital and productive to respond to various interventions.

As we learn more about the precise factors that control brain plasticity, we will be able to develop new approaches and to refine old ones. Instead of "new possibility," we can list the possibilities and provide a more rational plan of action. The pursuit of basic research and its applications will help find ways to make the brain more productive with aging.

REFERENCES

Anderson, K. J., Dam, D., & Cotman, C. (1988). Basic fibroblast growth factor prevents death of cholinergic neurons *in vivo*, *Nature, 33* (360–361).
Coleman, P. D., & Flood, D. G. (1986). Dendritic proliferation in the aging brain as a compensatory repair mechanism. *Progress in*

Brain Research, 70, 227–236 (D. F. Swaab, E. Fliers, M. Mirmiran, W. A. Van Gool, & F. Van Haaren, Eds., Elsevier Science Publ.).

Cotman, C. W., & Anderson, K. J. (1988). Synaptic plasticity and functional stabilization in the hippocampal formation: Possible role in Alzheimer's disease. In S. Waxman (Ed.), *Physiologic basis for functional recovery in neurological disease.* New York: Raven Press.

Cotman, C. W., & Lynch, G. (1987). The Neurobiology of learning and memory. *Learning Disabilities: Proceedings of the National Conference, January 12-13, 1987.*

Cotman, C. W., & Nieto-Sampedro, M. (1984). Cell biology of synaptic plasticity. *Science, 255,* 1287–1294.

Cotman, C. W., Nieto-Sampedro, M., & Harris, E. (1981). Synapse replacement in the nervous system of adult vertebrates. *Physiol. Reviews, 61,* 684–784.

Cotman, C. W., & Peterson, C. (1987). Aging. In Agranoff, B. W., Albers, R. W., Molinoff, P. B., & Siegel, G. (Eds.), *Basic neurochemistry.* NY: Raven Press.

Edds, M. V., Jr. (1953). Collateral nerve regeneration. *Q. Rev. Biol., 28,* 260–276.

Fischer, W., Wictorin, K., Bjorklund, A., Williams, L. R., Varon, S., & Gage, F. H. (1987). Amelioration of cholinergic neuron atrophy and spatial memory impairment in aged rats by nerve growth factor. *Nature, 329,* 65–68.

Geddes, J. W., Monaghan, D. T., Cotman, C. W., Lott, I. T., Kim, R. C., & Chui, H. C. (1985). Plasticity of hippocampal circuitry in Alzheimer's disease. *Science, 230,* 1179–1181.

Greenough, W. T. (1984). Structural correlates of information storage in the mammalian brain: A review and hypothesis. *Trends in Neuroscience 7*(7), 229–233.

Greenough, W. T., Larson, J. R., & Withers, G. S. (1985). Effects of unilateral and bilateral training in a reaching task on dendritic branching of neurons in the rat motor-sensory forelimb cortex. *Behav. Neural Biol., 44,* 301–314.

Hoff, S. F., Scheff, S. W., Benardo, L. S., & Cotman, C. W. (1982). Lesion-induced synaptogenesis in the dentate gyrus of aged rats: I. Loss and reaquisition of normal synaptic density. *J. Comp. Neurol., 205,* 246–252.

Hoffman, H. (1950). Local reinnervation in partially denervated muscle: A histophysiological study. *Aust. J. Exp. Biol. Med. Sci., 28,* 383–397.

Hyman, B. T., Van Hoesen, G. W., Damasio, A. R., & Barnes, C. L. (1984). Alzheimer's disease: Cell-specific pathology isolates the hippocampal formation. *Science, 225,* 1168–1170.

James, R., & Bradshaw, R. (1984). Polypeptide growth factors. *Annual Review of Biochemistry, 53,* 259–292.

Needels, D. L., Nieto-Sampedro, M., & Cotman, C. W. (1986). Induction of a neurite-promoting factor in rat brain following injury or deafferentation. *Neuroscience, 18,* 518–526.

Nieto-Sampedro, M., & Cotman, C. W. (1985). Growth factor induction and temporal order in CNS repair. In C. W. Cotman, (Ed.), *Synaptic plasticity.* New York: Guilford Press.

Nieto-Sampedro, M., Lewis, E. R., Cotman, C. W., Manthorpe, M., Skaper, S. D., Barbin, G., Longo, F. M., & Varon, S. (1982). Brain injury causes a time-dependent increase in neurotrophic activity at the lesion site. *Science, 217,* 860–861.

Nieto-Sampedro, M., Manthorpe, M., Barbin, G., Varon, S., & Cotman, C. W. (1983). Injury-induced neurotrophic activity in adult rat brain: Correlation with survival of delayed implants in the wound cavity. *J. Neurosci., 3* (11), 2219–2229.

Terry, R. D., DeTeresa, R., & Hansen, L. A. (1987). Neocortical cell counts in normal human adult aging. *Ann. Neurol., 21,* 530–539.

The Brain: Neurochemical Aspects

7

Shiganobu Nakamura

INTRODUCTION

The aging of the human brain is the most important of time's various effects because the aging of this organ or other associated systems produces personal suffering and family and societal difficulties. If the brain were capable of a long existence without loss of function, most, if not all, other bodily functions could probably be replaced—preferably by regenerating young cells or at worst by some mechanical means—and the individual could be said to survive.

However, nerve cells, the major functional component of the brain, are postmitotic and nondividing. They cannot regenerate after birth and are irreplaceable by other cells with similar functions.[1]

Functional recovery after brain damage has been a challenge to the orthodox concept of the "aging brain." Physiologically, it is unquestionable that the compensatory function of the brain can be ascribed to plastic changes in either or both synaptic transmission and neuronal connection. Recent electrophysiological and morphological studies (Foerster, 1982) have provided

[1] Compare with Carl Cotman's research results in preceding paper.

evidence for the occurrence of such changes during recovery after brain damage, although the causal relationship between each change and behavioral recovery is generally unclear. Chemically, a variety of substances have appeared as candidates responsible for the compensatory mechanism. These substances are called nerve growth factor (NGF) (Levi-Montalchini, Meyer, & Hamburger, 1954) or neurotrofic hormone (Appel, 1981). NGF has been shown to enhance the enzyme activity related to the acetylcholine synthesis (Honegger & Leonoir, 1982) or degradation (Lucas & Kreutzberg, 1985). Recently, much interest has been focused on acetylcholine metabolism because it may be associated with learning or memory (Drachman, 1977), and the lack of it may induce dementia (Perry & Perry, 1980).

The present paper will discuss the possibility of regulating neural functions damaged in the aging process through neurochemical methods, with emphasis on the acetylcholine neurotransmitter system.

REORGANIZATION OF NORMAL CIRCUITRIES

Kawaguchi and co-workers (1986) have recently given an insight into the mechanism of compensatory functioning from the standpoint of neurophysiology and neuroanatomy by investigating the regeneration of neuronal circuitries mainly in the cerebellum and related structures. In contrast to the previous concept of abortive regeneration of the mammalian central nervous tissues, occurrence of marked, functionally active regeneration of the projection from the cerebellum was proven in kittens after a complete transection of the projection.

Electrophysiological Studies

When the cerebellum of a normal kitten was stimulated by electric current, the electric response could be recorded at the frontal motor area of the cerebral cortex (Fig. 7.1A). The

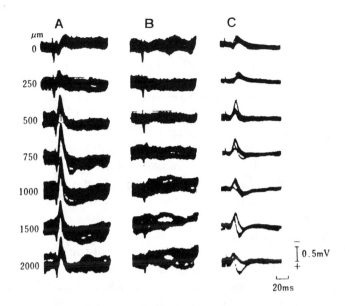

Figure 7.1. Functional connectivity of regenerated projections from the cerebellum. (*A*) The electric response in the frontal cortex obtained by the stimulus to the cerebellum of a normal kitten. (*B*) The disappearance of the response in the frontal cortex induced by transection of BCX. (*C*) The reappearance of the response in the frontal cortex after 19 days by the regeneration of the fiber from the cerebellum. (Kawaguchi et al., 1986)

transection—transverse cutting of the output fiber from the cerebellum, so-called brachium conjunctivum (BCX)—resulted in the disappearance of the response in the cerebral cortex (Fig. 7.1*B*). However, the regeneration of the fiber from the cerebellum to the cerebral cortex (BCX) resumed the electric response in the frontal cortex after 19 days (Fig. 7.1*C*) (Kawaguchi, Miyata, & Kato, 1986).

Morphological Studies

The damage to the cerebellum induced sprouting: a new growth of a spine-shaped structure in various collateral projections from the cerebellum. Marked regeneration of nerve fibers occurred after transection of the BCX. The elaborate technique using horseradish peroxidase demonstrated the origin, course, and destination of the regenerated fibers after BCX transection. Most of the regenerated fibers took a course similar to that of the normal projection and terminated in the normal projection areas (Kawaguchi et al., 1986).

Newly formed connections, either by collateral sprouting or regeneration of nerve fibers, became active in a time course much slower than that of the learning process. These connections may contribute to the recovery of function after injuries to nervous tissues.

At least three fundamentally different mechanisms can be considered for the compensatory function of the brain. The first is a mechanism that begins to work immediately after damage to the brain, possibly by opening previously inactive pathways as in the switching of communication lines. This appears to work in emergencies and is replaced gradually by the second mechanism, presumably a process similar to learning. The third is a mechanism that induces a marked reorganization of neuronal circuitries by the sprouting or regeneration of nerve fibers. This mechanism begins to work in a time course much slower than the learning process, although evidence is unclear as to its contribution to functional recovery.

ACETYLCHOLINE

Acetylcholine is proposed as an important neurotransmitter for mental functions such as memory or learning. It is produced by acetyl-CoA, derived from glucose and choline transported to the brain. The enzyme, choline acetyltransferase (ChAT), is necessary for the reaction. When stimuli reach the nerve terminal, acetylcholine is released from the terminal and transmits the stimuli to the neighboring nerve cell by binding to the receptor. Then acetylcholine is degraded to choline and acetic acid by acetylcholinesterase (AChE) (Fig. 7.2).

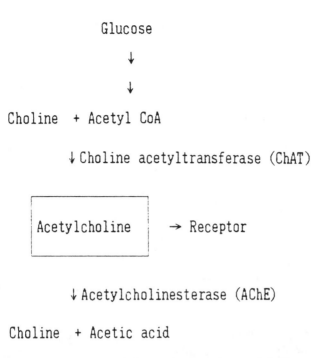

Figure 7.2. Biosynthesis and degradation of acetylcholine.

Age-Related Changes in Acetylcholine

Choline acetyltransferase (ChAT) activity was measured in the cerebrospinal fluid of subjects who were free of any central nervous system (CNS) disease. The ChAT activity in the cerebrospinal fluid decreased mildly with increasing age (Fig. 7.3). The ChAT activity has been reported to also decrease in various parts of the cerebral cortex of the autopsied brain (McGeer & McGeer, 1976).

The activity of AChE, the degradative enzyme, increased in the cerebrospinal fluid of control subjects in contrast to ChAT activity (Fig. 7.4) (Nakano, Kato, Nakamura, & Kameyama, 1986). The decrease in production and the increase in breakdown may cause the reduction of acetylcholine content in the brain of the aged.

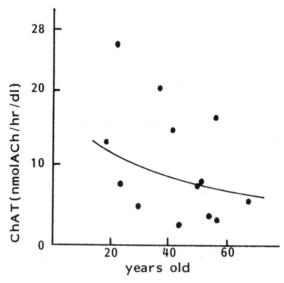

Figure 7.3. Age-related decrease in ChAT activity in the cerebrospinal fluid of control subjects.

Changes in Acetylcholine in Patients with Alzheimer-Type Dementia

The Alzheimer-type dementia is a degenerative disease characterized by a progressive mental deterioration. The incidence of the Alzheimer-type dementia increases with advanced age. Thus, Alzheimer-type dementia will be one of the heaviest burdens for the future society which will have a high proportion of elderly.

The activity of ChAT was reduced in all measured areas of the cerebral cortex and in the nucleus basalis of Meynert of the autopsied brain obtained from patients with Alzheimer-type dementia (Fig. 7.5) (Nakamura et al., 1984). The nucleus basalis of Meynert is made up of large nerve cells containing acetylcholine and projects fibers to the cerebral cortex. Whitehouse and co-workers (1982) have suggested the importance of cell loss in the nucleus basalis of Meynert as a cause of Alzheimer-type dementia.

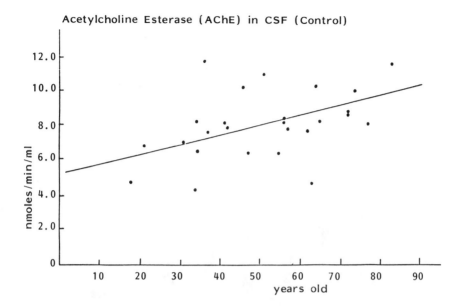

Figure 7.4. Age-related increase in AChE activity in the cerebrospinal fluid of control subjects. (Koshimura et al., 1987)

The decrease in ChAT activity was more pronounced in the early onset of Alzheimer-type dementia (Perry, Gibson, Blessed, Perry, & Tomlinson, 1977) than in the late onset (Koshimura, Kato, Tohyama, Nakamura, & Kameyama, 1987). The former has been called Alzheimer's disease and is distinguished from the latter (senile dementia) by rapid progress and a variety of symptoms such as aphasia, apraxia, or raphia.

ChAT activities in autopsied brains were inversely related with the frequency of morphologically abnormal structures specific to Alzheimer-type dementia, such as senile plaque or Alzheimer neurofibrillary tangles (Perry et al., 1978). ChAT in the brain of patients with Alzheimer-type dementia showed a decrease in number and also a change in characteristics (Koshimura, Kato, Tohyama, Nakamura, & Kameyama, 1986). The remaining ChAT showed a low affinity to choline or to acetyl-CoA, suggesting the decreased efficiency of the enzyme.

Acetylcholine is bound to two types of receptors, muscarinic

CAT ACTIVITY OF AUTOPSY BRAIN

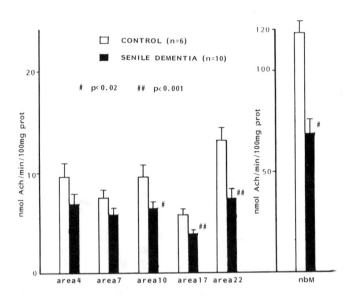

Figure 7.5. ChAT activity in the autopsied brain of patients with Alzheimer-type dementia with late onset (senile dementia). nbM: nucleus basalis of Meynert. (Nakamura & Kameyama, 1986)

and nicotinic. The number of muscarinic receptors is reduced in the nucleus basalis of Meynert and in the hippocampus of Alzheimer-type dementia (Fig. 7.6) (Shimohama, Taniguchi, Fujiwara, & Kameyama, 1986.) The nicotinic receptor is also decreased in number in the nucleus basalis of Meynert and in the putamen (Fig. 7.7).

 AChE activity was significantly ($p < .05$) lower in the cerebrospinal fluid of patients with rapidly progressive Alzheimer's disease compared with age-matched control subjects (Fig. 7.8) (Nakamura & Kameyama, 1986). However, AChE activity in the cerebrospinal fluid showed a wide variation among patients with slow progressive senile dementia. The less severely demented cases tend to have higher levels of AChE activity than more mentally impaired patients.

AChE activity was also demonstrated histochemically in the

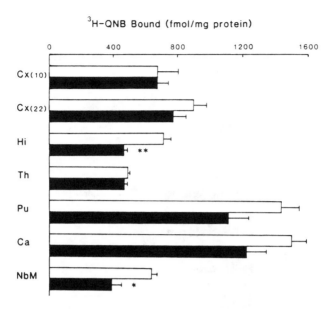

Figure 7.6. Muscarinic receptor in the brain of control and Alzheimer-type dementia patients. The number of receptors was measured by the specific binding of ^{3}H-QNB. (Nakano et al., 1986) (Control: Alzheimer-type dementia) Cx(10):frontal lobe; Cx(22):temporal lobe; Hi:hippocampus; Th:thalamus; Pu:putamen; Ca:caudate; NbM:nucleus basalis of Meynert.

human autopsied brain. AChE activity was strongly positive in the core of the senile plaque in the brain of the patient with Alzheimer-type dementia (Perry, 1980). The core of the senile plaque has been reported by the histochemical methods to also contain somatostatin or neuropeptide Y (Nakamura & Vincent, 1986).

These results suggest that the level of AChE could be elevated in the early stage of the disease (Summers, Majovski, Marsh, Tachiki, & Kling, 1986) and may reflect reactive pathological changes in the central cholinergic systems. Increase of the cerebrospinal fluid AChE with age might arise from a similar mechanism. That is, a mild degradation on acetylcholine-related system may cause the elevated level of AChE.

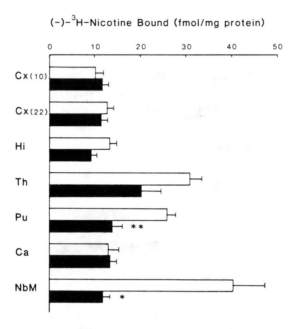

Figure 7.7. Nicotinic receptor in the brain of control and Alzheimer-type dementia patients. The number of receptors was measured by the specific binding of (–)–^{3}H-nicotine. (Nakano et al., 1986) (Control: Alzheimer-type dementia)

MEDICAL TRIALS THROUGH PLASTICITY

Strangely, few attempts were carried out to prevent or alleviate suffering caused by the pathological aging of the brain. This resigned attitude was especially remarkable in Japan, since the decrement of intellect in the aged was regarded as a preparatory stage before death because it eased the fear of death. However, recent changes in the family system and in the number of the aged in Japan have brought about severe social and economical obstacles by pathological changes in the aged brain. Under these circumstances, medical and paramedical managements are also strongly demanded in Japan. Although medical trials are very difficult and cannot be called fully successful, some seem to be promising and may break through to a new possibility.

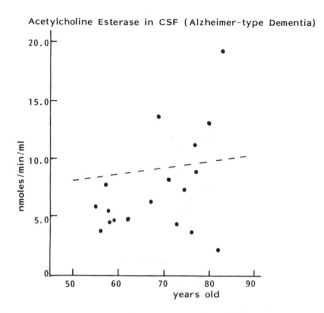

Figure 7.8. AChE activity in the cerebrospinal fluid of patients with Alzheimer-type dementia. Dashed line shows the regression line obtained from control subjects (Fig. 7.4).

THERAPY THROUGH ACETYLCHOLINE

Summers and co-workers (1986) administered the combination of an acetylcholine precursor, lecithin, and an AChE inhibitor, tetrahydroaminoacridine, to patients with Alzheimer-type dementia through the increase in acetylcholine content in their brains. They reported an improvement in intelligent in 16 out of 17 cases of Alzheimer-type dementia (Fig. 7.9).

The AChE inhibitor, physostigmine, was also administered to a 63-year-old patient with Alzheimer's disease, and we examined his mental test score (Table 7.1). The administration of the placebo resulted in a slight improvement in his mental test score. The injection of physostigmine, however, unexpectedly lowered the score; further addition of it worsened it. After intermission of the drug, his mental score returned to the pretreatment level. The activity of AChE was decreased in his cerebrospinal fluid.

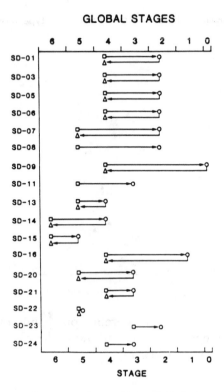

Figure 7.9. Change in stage (severity) of Alzheimer-type dementia during oral treatment with tetrahydroaminoacridine. The squares denote the pretreatment stage, the circles the effect of the drug, and the triangles the placebo effect. (Shimohama et al., 1986)

These results indicate that the therapeutic window of the drug is very narrow, and the overdose of the drug easily causes the adverse effect. Thus, the dosage should be carefully determined in the light of AChE activity in the plasma or cerebrospinal fluid.

TRANSPLANTING OF NEURAL TISSUES

Another important aspect of the plasticity of the brain is the transplanting of neural tissues. Since the nerve cell is

Table 7.1. Physostigmine (AChE Inhibitor) Administration to a 63-Year-Old Patient with Alzheimer-Type Dementia

Treatment	Mental Test Score[a]
Before trial	81
Placebo (saline)	100.5
Physostigmine (1.0 mg)	58
Physostigmine (1.0 mg)	30
After trial	83

[a] Full mark: 125.

postmitotic and nondividing, the transplanting of young cells can be expected to produce renewed activity.

Although the history of experiments on neural transplants is old, the number of publications on them is increasing rapidly. In actuality, the neural transplant technique is not complicated, since the brain is an immunologically privileged site.

Cultured nerve cells obtained from the spinal cord of a monkey could be transplanted into the lateral ventricle of a rat (Kamo, 1987). Immunohistochemical staining with lectin showed the growth of the dendrite of transplanted cells into the cerebral cortex of the rat brain, suggesting neural activity by newly transplanted cells.

Kamo and co-workers (1986) transplanted sympathetic ganglion cells or adrenal cells, prepared with a treatment of a toxin, 6-hydroxydopamine, into model rats with Parkinson's disease. Abnormal movement, such as rotation, decreased in the rats with the transplants, as compared with the control rats (Fig. 7.10). These procedures may provide a new approach to future productive aging.

CONCLUSION

Various new techniques are being developed but may involve new medical side effects or ethical problems. We scientists must always be aware that every researcher can become a Dr. Frankenstein through adventurous biotechnology.

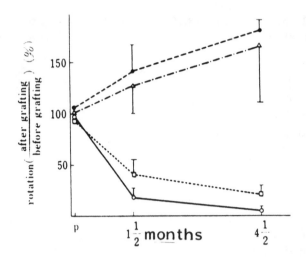

Figure 7.10. Effect of transplantation on rat model of Parkinson's disease. p:pretreatment; ●:unsuccessful transplantation; ○:successful transplantation of synpathetic ganglion cells; □:successful transplantation of adrenal chromaffin cells; △:controls. (Summers et al., 1986)

In contrast, old Japanese people like the Noh dance-drama (Fig. 7.11), which requires a skillful performance and memory of the music and text. Both the behavioral and mental training may keep neuronal circuitries intact by constant nervous stimuli to the receptor. A Noh play is safer and less expensive than elegant drugs or transplants. In my opinion, a Noh play or its equivalent will promise productive aging for healthy elderly. However, when they fall into a pathological condition, drugs or other appropriate medical methods will be available at the early stages to prevent its / = \\ progression and to cure the deterioration, which will also lead to productive aging.

ACKNOWLEDGMENTS

I wish to thank Dr. M. Kameyama, Sumitomo Hospital, Osaka; Dr. S. Kawaguchi, Institute for Brain Research, Faculty

Figure 7.11. A 71-year old Japanese female in a Noh play.

of Medicine, Kyoto University; and Drs. T. Kato, H. Kamo, S. Nakamura, K. Koshimura, S. Shimohama, and S. Nakano, Department of Neurology, Kyoto University Hospital, for their valuable help and advice.

REFERENCES

Appel, S. H. (1981). A unifying hypothesis for the cause of amyotrophic lateral sclerosis, Parkinsonism, and Alzheimer's disease. *Ann. Neurol., 10,* 499–505.

Atack, J. R., Perry, E. K., Perry, R. H., Wilson, I. D., Bober, M. J., Blessed, G., & Tomlinson, B. E. (1985). Blood acetyl- and butyryl-choline-sterases in senile dementia of Alzheimer type. *J. Neurol. Sci., 70,* 1–12.

Drachman, D. A. (1977). Cognitive function in man. Does the cholinergic system have a special role? *Neurology, 27,* 783–790.

Foerster, A. P. (1982). Spontaneous regeneration of cut axons in adult rat brain. *J. Comp. Neurol., 210,* 335–356.

Honegger, H., & Leonoir, D. (1982). Nerve growth factor (NGF) stimulation of cholinergic telencephalic neurons in aggregating cell cultures. *Dev. Brain Res., 3,* 229–238.

Kamo, H. (1987). Neural transplantation. In M. Kameyama (Ed.), *Geriatric Neurology —Update,* 441–444.

Kamo, H., Kim, S. O., McGeer, P. L., & Shin, D. H. (1986). Functional recovery in a rat model of Parkinson's disease following transplantation of cultured human sympathetic neurons. *Brain Res., 397,* 372–376.

Kawaguchi, S., Miyata, H., & Kato, N. (1986). Regeneration of the cerebellofugal projection after transection of the superior cerebellar peduncle in kittens: Morphological and electrophysiological studies. *J. Comp. Neurol., 245,* 258–273.

Koshimura, K., Kato, T., Tohyama, I., Nakamura, S., & Kameyama, M. (1986). Qualitative abnormalities of choline acetyltransferase in Alzheimer type dementia. *J. Neurol. Sci., 76,* 143–150.

Koshimura, K., Kato, T., Tohyama, I., Nakamura, S., & Kameyama, M. (1987). Correlation of choline acetyltransferase activity between the nucleus basalis of Meynert and the cerebral cortex. *Neurosci. Res., 4,* 330–336.

Levi-Montalchini, R., Meyer, H., & Hamburger, V. (1954). In vitro experiments on the effects of mouse sarcomas 180 and 37 on the spinal and sympathetic ganglia of the chick embryo. *Cancer Res., 14,* 49–57.

Lucas, C. A., & Kreutzberg, G. W. (1985). Regulation of acetylcholinesterase secretion from neuronal cell cultures. 1. Actions of nerve growth factor, cytoskeletal inhibitors and Tunicamycin. *Neuro. Sci., 14,* 349–360.

McGeer, E., & McGeer, P. L. (1976). Neurotransmitter metabolism in the aging brain. In R. D. Terry & S. Gershon (Eds.), *Neurobiology of aging* (pp. 389–403). New York: Raven Press.

Nakamura, S., & Kameyama, M. (1986). Aging and neurotransmitters. *Jpn. J. Med., 25,* 87–89.

Nakamura, S., Koshimura, K., Kato, T., Yamao, S., Iijima, S., Nagata, H., Miyata, S., Fujiiyoshi, K., Okamoto, K., Suga, H., & Kameyama, M. (1984). Neurotransmitters in dementia. *Clin. Therap., 7,* 18–34.

Nakamura, S., & Vincent, S. R. (1986). Somatostatin and neuropeptide Y-immunoreactive neurons in the neocortex in senile dementia of Alzheimer type. *J. Neurol. Sci., 70,* 11–20.

Nakano, S., Kato, T., Nakamura, S., & Kameyama, M. (1986). Acetylcholine-sterase activity in cerebrospinal fluid of patients with Alzheimer's disease and senile dementia. *J. Neurol. Sci., 75,* 213–223.

Perry, E. K. (1980). The cholinergic system in old age and Alzheimer's disease. *Age and Aging, 9,* 1–8.

Perry, E. K., Gibson, P. H., Blessed, G., Perry, R. H., & Tomlinson, B. E. (1977). Neurotransmitter enzyme abnormalities in senile dementia—Choline acetyltransferase and glutamic acid decarboxylase activities in necropsy brain tissue. *J. Neurol. Sci., 34,* 247–265.

Perry, E. K., & Perry, R. H. (1980). The cholinergic system in Alzheimer's disease. In P. J. Roberts (Ed.), *Biochemistry of dementia* (pp. 135–183). Chichester, England: Wiley.

Perry, R. H., Tomlinson, B. E., Blessed, G., Bergman, K., Gibson, P. H., & Perry, R. H. (1978). Correlation of cholinergic abnormalities with senile plaques and mental test scores in senile dementia. *Br. Med. J., 2,* 1457–1459.

Shimohama, S., Taniguchi, T., Fujiwara, M., & Kameyama, M. (1986). Acetylcholine receptors in Alzheimer-type dementia. In H. Yoshida (Ed.), *Recent research on neurotransmitter receptors* (pp. 2–12). Amsterdam, The Netherlands: Excerpta Medica.

Summers, W. K., Majovski, L. V., Marsh, G. M., Tachiki, K., & Kling, A. (1986). Oral tetrahydroaminoacridine in long-term treatment of senile dementia. *N. Engl. J. Med., 315,* 1241–1245.

Whitehouse, P. J., Price, D. L., Struble, R. G., Clark, A. W., Coyle, J. J., & DeLong, M. R. (1982). Loss of neurons in the basal forebrain. *Science, 215,* 1237–1239.

Concluding Discussion 8

LED BY ALVAR SVANBORG

We Swedes live longer than any Scandinavian population today. In fact, we are still the oldest country in the world as far as the percentage of elderly in the total population is concerned. At present, approximately 17% of Swedes are 65 and above, and as far as we can predict today, in the year 2020 it will be closer to one-fourth than one-fifth.

I would like to briefly describe some of the results obtained in our longitudinal studies in Goteborg, Sweden, begun in 1971 to 1972. I emphasize that the group we have studied is not a very rich, well-educated, or special one by any means, but rather is representative of the total population.

The first-age cohort, born in 1901 to 1902, has been followed for 15 years, up to the age of 85. The other cohort, born 5 years later, 1906 to 1907, has been followed up to age 79. Because of their rather marked age cohort differences, we added a third cohort, born 10 years after the first, 1911 to 1912. To that age cohort we have added an intervention program. We have tried to improve the life of the 70-year-olds for 2-year periods in order to test different ideas we have had concerning influences upon aging—to see if we could positively influence the rate of aging and state of health.

Let me say two things about these three age cohorts. The first concerns the plasticity of aging. We have generally thought that either we grow old and mature or we start a downhill decline for the rest of our lives. This is not true. Of course, some functions begin to decrease almost immediately after the growing phase; however, many other functions remain astonishingly unchanged as far as we can measure, where the rate of measurable decline is postponed until the age of 70 or 75.

Secondly, we are astonished to find that there can be both downhill and uphill periods, even if, over the long run, there is a decrease in function. For example, we have fast-reacting and slow-reacting muscle fibers. The fast-reacting do grow old faster than the slow-reacting ones, but we have found that today, even at the age of 81 years of age, it is possible through training to improve not only muscle strength, but also the composition and efficacy of muscle fibers. A Stockholm physiologist who has followed the trainability of younger people recently stated, in comparison with our studies, that the percentage increased by training at 81 apparently is the same as the percentage increased at 30. Obviously, the same level of performance is not reached, but the trainability is still there. We've heard that we could not slow down the skeleton's aging rate, but we have some data indicating that this is not true. Even if the density of the skeleton can't be improved, the rate of decline can be slowed down. This must be a general biological phenomenon. Our cells are stimulated by use. The problem, of course, is that the older one becomes, the less his or her reserve capacity and the greater the risk of overload. But the wide range between stimulation and overload is astonishing.

The other interesting plasticity we have found is age cohort differences, meaning that today's 70-year-olds generally are healthier and more vital than 70-year-olds just 10 years ago. These differences concern not only the fewer occurrences of lung cancer or other disorders, but also, as far as we can measure, the rate and consequences of those processes we use to identify the aging process. We've always believed that genetic factors were the main determinants for the rate and functional consequences of aging, but we cannot see that any migration has occurred in the population of Goteborg, Sweden, that could help explain a change in the genetic base. Thus, we conclude that as far as we can see, life-style and environmental factors must play a much greater role than we had previously thought— not only concerning the state of health, but also the rate and functional consequences of aging. For example, smoking not only causes higher risks of lung cancer and alcohol abuse higher risks of liver cirrhosis, but they also obviously accelerate the rate of aging. For instance, the density of the skeleton of a 70-year-old smoker in Sweden is, on the average, around 25% less than a 70-year-old nonsmoker. By studying the production in the gonadals of female and male sex hormones, we have also found that smokers and alcohol abusers grow old faster. For example, a smoking female in Goteborg today reaches menopause 2 years earlier than nonsmokers.

Finally, I would like to mention studies on bereavement, also performed in this country. It has long been known that people who lose their spouses have shorter life expectancies. We have been mainly interested in the rather dramatic change during the three first months of loneliness. In Sweden today, a male who has lost his spouse increases his risk of dying by at least 48% during the first three months. For females it is 22%. When we look at the immune response in this situation, we find that it's not only the risk of falling, the risk of committing suicide, and the risk of being killed as a pedestrian in the streets that increase during these first three months of loneliness, but physiological aging also accelerates during this stress situation.

QUESTIONER: Has your study shown anything about the effect remarriage has after the loss of a spouse?

SVANBORG: One of the reasons why we started between 50 and 90 is that most people remarry before 50. In Sweden, men remarry also after the age of 50, females astonishingly seldom. We have also compared 360,000 widows with the rest of the population over a 10-year period. Living together also exists in Sweden. So I cannot really answer your question.

QUESTIONER: Dr. Cotman, you mentioned the advances due to more sophisticated computer uses. Now there are experiments that are optical/neural. My question is twofold: (1) Do you see further advances coming back to brain research from these advances in computer sciences which have, in some sense, come from the brain research field? And (2) in terms of the convergences, what kind of communication—and this would also go to Dr. Nakamura—between the two fields do you see formally arising that will accelerate?

COTMAN: That's an excellent question and statement at the same time. I guess you'd technically call it "reverse engineering," that you're applying some brain principles to computers, but at the same time you end up with more real models of the nervous system. Frankly, I think that's a welcome relief because some of the interactions at the neurotransmitter level are so complex now that one can really not intuit fully the meaning of some of the plastic adaptations that take place. So we are now actively working with many programmers and trying to bring young engineers into the neural sciences to help us use more accurate animal models. In turn, what you find from using animal models are testable predictions. That's really the point of a model. If it tells you something you already knew, it's not really a good model. But you find unexpected variables coming out that are particularly exciting. Many different programs are being started at various universities throughout the country to bring together engineers and neuroscientists.

NAKAMURA: A computer could be a very useful model for memory or other kinds of brain functioning, but we must be aware that we have emotions that influence memory. What is very interesting is that we can memorize quite easily, but if it's unpleasant, we forget quite easily. A computer, however, does not have such emotions and that is the difference. A computer can approximate the human brain, but not completely.

SVANBORG: May I ask a question to the two of you? Longitudinally, I think it's interesting to find that the psychomotor speed,

at least among Swedes, seems to start to go down already somewhere between the ages of 23 to 25, at the same time as measurable cognitive abilities are showing either a plateau or an
increase. Is dopamine content going down in caudate nucleus
at a different rate than psychomotor speed? There seems to be a
discrepancy, and this is important because it's often a reason
for misdiagnosis of senile dementia. Also, people who are able
to cope rather well intellectually may have such a slow speed—
especially when they are tired or when they have an infection.
Could you explain this discrepancy? Is it just that the lowering
of psychomotor speed is a consequence of the accumulation of
more and more variables in the brain? The neuroconductor
speed is going down only 8% over the life-span.

COTMAN: I think there's another area where, in the life history
of these systems, we can use more information, but it appears
as if there are different systems serving different types of learning. For example, learning skills like riding a bicycle or typing
are known to use a circuit in the brain different from that
involved in something like learning lists. The latter drops out
much more easily with aging, and the neurons are more vulnerable. It's almost as if there's a plasticity that if you push too
hard, it finally does get taxed and is unable to withstand it. On
the other hand, the former system seems to show some early
decrements, but then it stays remarkably stable, even in
Alzheimer's disease.

QUESTIONER: During World War II, some doctors studying the
impact of shrapnel wounds in brain-damaged soldiers discovered
that they could, through therapy, reprogram portions of the damaged brain. They eventually formed the Institute for the Rehabilitation of the Brain-Injured in Philadelphia and applied what they
had learned during the war to help children who were brain damaged at birth or through illness. I wonder if Dr. Cotman knows of
this institute and of the work these people have done for the past
40 years to help many people reprogram their brains and perform better. Also, I wonder if some of this experience and knowledge could be applied to the elderly.

COTMAN: Interesting question. This is called shaping, isn't it?

QUESTIONER: Patterning.

COTMAN: Patterning, sorry. Yes, I'm familiar with it. In fact, one of my graduate students has practiced this on her daughter for the last several years; thus, we will have somebody in the basic science program who has gone through much of this. I think it's too early yet to tell, but certainly with brain circuitry there are recovery mechanisms, as we have indicated, and also alternative circuits that can pick up function. These can be put into more use, particularly in children, when the system is more plastic. I think our thinking about it ends with younger persons, but now we know that this plasticity continues on into old age. How much of this can really be applied remains to be determined, but it's an exciting possibility.

SVANBORG: In our age cohort comparisons we have found an ongoing positive trend in intellectual capacity, a trend that, as far as we understand, cannot be explained by any methodological differences. Thus, the elderly of today are significantly intellectually more capable than the elderly of 10 years ago. Similar studies have been going on in this country revealing the same results. We had hoped that this would be a basis also for a lowering of the incidence of senile dementia, but as far as we can see now, we have no indication of this.

COTMAN: Dr. Svanborg, you mentioned you were looking into various interventions over a 2-year period. I'm curious as to what types of interventions you particularly are betting on, or do you have data that seem to underlie some of these trends and improvements?

SVANBORG: When you compare, for example, intellectual functioning in the elderly, so many have socially isolated lives, especially the females, and their intellectual–physical activity is so low. We have tried to improve that. We have to try to stimulate them in different ways, physically, intellectually, and also emotionally. Over a period of 2 years, we have measured rates, stem function, auditory and visceral response, cerebral blood flow—

so many different things. Our aim is to see to what extent training improves not only the muscles but also intellectual capacity, even when training starts as late as the age of 70.

BUTLER: This fascinating material regarding plasticity gives us great hope and makes quite clear that productivity is essential to human health. Without providing an opportunity to be productive, we condemn the human being to becoming dysfunctional and aged, in a traditional sense. Perhaps the policies of premature retirement in themselves have become directives for premature aging.

Cultural, Social, Economic, and Political Implications of Productive Aging

Can We Extend the Work Life?

9

INTRODUCTION TO CHAPTER 9

The Japanese and American contributors in this chapter represent several key perspectives on productive aging: labor, government, business, and health care. They demonstrate that there is, indeed, no shortage of ideas on ways in which society can adjust to the longevity revolution by extending the work life.

Both countries display many mixed messages on productive aging. Transitions to employment policy cognizant of the resourcefulness of the elderly worker population are occurring unevenly and haltingly. We see more sensitivity to the waste of human capital, the undermining of health and spirit, and destitution stemming from the exclusion of willing and able older people from the work force. Trends of early retirement seem to continue, used by management to thin out the work force in lean times and by workers to escape from hostile managements.

The contributors deal with the potentials for extending the work life, and the conditions and opportunities under which the extension can be realized. The discussion of options takes us beyond the later years: Productive-aging policy, it appears, requires attention to life-cycle needs, retraining, health promotion, the changing economy and demographics, and technology.

A driving force for these considerations is the shortage of younger workers following the enormous postwar birth cohorts.

Technology offers an example of an industrial factor that can cut two ways, unless directed by circumspect policy making: It can promote extended work life by allowing flexibility in absorbing elderly and other workers with physical and mental limitations. But technology also may bring pressures for reducing the work force if more wealth can be produced by fewer workers. And these pressures may be expressed discriminatorily against older workers. Improved national productivity might be directed toward more leisure time, more education, and better financial and service benefits for the elderly and the working family members who care for the frail and children. There are obvious intergenerational repercussions to policies of productive aging.

A consensus exists among contributors for a diversity of options, including voluntary as well as paid activity, and flexibility in the timing of retirement. Workers should neither be forced out of work or forced to keep on working. The notion of partial retirement is implicit in several presentations. If society embraces productive aging as a goal, fundamental questions must be asked, as some of the speakers do, about employer willingness to make careful assessments of worker capabilities in relation to work assignments, and policy on reward, advancement, and job conditions. Many current policies give the message that older people are marginal and expendable. It is a message that none of the contributors will accept.

Extended Work Life Opportunities and Obstacles

Tadashi Nakamura

THE GROWING ELDERLY

Due to both a sharp drop in the birth rate and a rise in life expectancy, the elderly population has grown remarkably in recent decades. Added to this, increased availability of higher education and their willingness to work have considerably increased the percentage of elderly in the total work force. Over the last 15 years, the elderly work force has grown by 3 million, constituting one-sixth of the total work force; 60% of these are between the ages of 55 and 59. It is estimated that in the next 15 years, it will grow another 4 million; 30% will be aged 60 to 65 and 40% will be 65 and older. The elderly will then occupy one-quarter of the total work force. It is unfortunate, however, that the elderly have the highest unemployment rate. Due to cost factors and adaptability, the larger the company and tighter the labor market, the more employers tend to recruit younger applicants, particularly recent graduates.

GUARANTEEING WORK FOR THE ELDERLY

After the Korean War, the economy recovered and grew until the first oil crisis, indicating an improved labor market.

However, because job opportunities were scarce for middle-aged and older workers, the government provided special counseling services and retraining opportunities.

Around the mid- 1960s, the labor market situation became more imbalanced with a continued shortage of younger skilled workers and a tight labor market in urban areas on the one hand and a surplus of middle-aged and older workers in rural areas on the other. According to social consensus, the extension of the retirement age from the usual age 55 became a "must." The need of guaranteeing work opportunities for those between 60 and 65 had to be met by extending the employment and/or reemployment system. Additionally, retirement age and voluntary participation in social activities for those past 65 had to be assured.

To control this situation, various laws were revised and enacted between 1966 and 1974 to implement an active manpower policy and promote reinsertion of older workers. They adjusted the seniority wage and promotion system and advocated that employers set a fixed retirement age and incorporate lump-sum retirement allowances. The Silver Manpower Center was founded to provide clearing services for short-term and supplementary work for those over 60 still willing to work. By 1986, two-thirds of companies had set or planned to set the retirement age at 60 or older.

For various reasons, government has realized a 60-year retirement age objective through a consensus method, rather than placing a legal obligation on the part of employers:

1. The age of the work force and the age at which the workers retire vary considerably by industry and size of individual companies.
2. Raising the retirement age has to be accompanied by modifications of seniority wages and a promotion system as well as lump-sum retirement allowances which are negotiable issues.
3. Though a majority of the elderly are engaged in permanent work, many, especially females, work on a part-time basis. The older the worker, the more he or she tends to choose less restrictive types of work. This also applies to those not presently working, but who wish to do so.
4. The older the worker, the more the degree of willingness to work

varies per individual, dependent upon health conditions and sources of other income.

CONCLUSIONS

It is important to note four future possibilities:

1. Although over the past 15 years the younger labor force (19 to 25) has decreased by 4 million, it is anticipated to grow by 2 million in the next 15 years as the children of the baby boomers join the labor market. This implies that employers will rely more on young applicants rather than on the elderly in filling vacancies.
2. The number of women in the work force will continue to grow, but to a lesser degree both in volume and speed than in the last decade. They, too, compete with the elderly in the labor market, as both tend to find employment in the tertiary sector and choose part-time jobs.
3. Faced with an uncertain exchange rate, pressure for protection in world trade, and a possible low growth of economy, employees presently feel that redundancy in their enterprise is unbearable and adjustment of employment is unavoidable.
4. Pension systems are not expected to be expanded due to a government budget deficit and an upsurge of the elderly population.

In light of present and future situations, all possible means have to be applied to guarantee work opportunities for the elderly so that their willingness to participate in social activities is satisfied and their participation will contribute to economic growth, social stability, and personal well-being.

In this connection, three major instruments must be mentioned: first, life-long education and training to enable working people to adapt to changing job descriptions and to participate positively in social activities in later stages of their working lives; secondly, a shortening of working hours to provide time to pursue training for working people and create wide opportunities for part-time jobs for the elderly; finally, a life-long health plan to enable workers to participate in work and other social activities, particularly during later life.

The Aging of the Labor Force in Japan

Takao Komine

As the 21st century approaches and the baby boomers reach retirement age, Japan will become the most aged society. Securing employment opportunities for those elderly who can and want to work will be necessary to both help relieve the burden placed on younger workers and make the elderly feel useful.

To accomplish this, we must first understand that our labor force will be older than that of other countries because we will have the highest average age and the highest rate of elderly participation in the labor force. Even now, we have a higher number of people past 55 who are employed or seeking employment; the difference is even greater for those 65 and over: 37% for Japanese males but less than 20% for American males. In the future, this rate will fall due to such things as increased income and improvements in the social security system. But although a 32.7% rate is projected for the year 2000, our rate will still be higher. The percentage of those over 60 in the total labor force was 9.8% in 1985 and expected to reach 13.6% in 2000.

Considering the future labor market situation, it will be difficult to secure adequate employment opportunities for the elderly. Besides the rapid increase in the number of people reaching retirement age, many firms will be forced to restructure their businesses or relocate their factories to foreign countries due to the

116

increased value of the yen and growing international competition. Older workers will be laid off first because their wages are much higher under the Japanese seniority-based system, and they are considered less able than younger workers to adapt to the new economic environment. Those laid off from long-term jobs will have trouble finding new jobs, for firms prefer to employ and offer on-the-job training for younger workers. Since most training is firm specific, older workers trained by one firm are not in demand by others.

But we also should look at the bright side. Two factors may remove barriers blocking older workers from getting new jobs. First is the enlargement of service industries. In 1980, 44.2% of the total labor force was engaged in service industries; this is expected to increase to 52% in the year 2000. Physical productivity is less important in service industries than in manufacturing. Also, it is likely that service industries will create flexible employment opportunities such as flex-time or part-time jobs suited to older workers.

The second factor is technological progress. As the number of older workers increases, competition will emerge among firms concerned with how to best use these workers. Hopefully, technology will be developed that makes work easier for them and allows full use of their abilities.

Along with an increase in employment opportunities for older workers, we should adopt what I call Japanese-style work sharing which aims at creating greater employment opportunities for older people by reducing the working hours of younger workers. In view of trade friction, this should stimulate domestic demand to reduce external imbalance. Reduction of working hours would foster household consumption.

To implement this, we must encourage promotion of the five-day week, life-time education, and job creation for older workers. In addition, changes in Japanese employment practices such as seniority-based wages and life-time employment should be long-term goals.

A Multiindustry Career to Extend Work Life

Sumio Yoshida

I am happy to congratulate the older American worker for getting back the right to work. It is meaningful and useful for older people to be in the work force, not only economically, but also medically and socially.

Can we extend the work life? The answer is obviously yes, but perspectives vary between government and corporate policymakers.

As the President of Japan's Well-Aging Association, established in 1953, I believe that later life must be not only productive, but also healthy and fulfilling. With this belief, I present a concept that encourages older people to combine their industrial or service careers with farming, providing future generations with a nonpolluted natural environment. Before elaborating on this, I must first briefly outline the current economic conditions in Japan against which the proposed concept was developed.

Even though the retirement age has been extended to 60 years and older in the majority of Japanese firms, actual job availability for older people is not promising, particularly in the manufacturing industries. First, advanced mechanization has cut down the work force in many industries. Second, the participation of women and older workers in the labor force has increased rapidly in the last decade, making employment more competitive. Third, Japan's sluggish domestic market and

118

stagnant export market are squeezing many corporations' profit margins and causing the nation's unemployment rate to near 3%. Thus, employment opportunities for older people will be tighter and early retirement will become more common. Although recognizing the constraints Japanese businesses face, we feel that these developments are detrimental to a "productive, healthy, and fulfilling" later life.

On the other hand, the multi-industry career concept will provide adequate work opportunities for older workers. It is a radical version of flex-time job arrangement. Under this scheme, when a worker reaches retirement age, he continues to work at the same work place, but only for several months a year, spending the remaining time on a farm. The degree of involvement in farming can vary, depending upon his or her agricultural expertise, as well as financial and physical abilities.

This proposal has at least three obvious merits. (1) Reduced months at industrial or service jobs will increase job opportunities for others. (2) Since many jobs in the modern factory and office are mentally stressful, farming, which can be recreational and restorative, will provide a welcome change. (3) Many able-bodied men have left Japanese villages to seek urban employment, resulting in extensive deteriorating farm acreage.

Of course, this proposal contains several problems that need to be dealt with before it can become workable. How will the factory adjust to a fluctuating labor supply that reflects fluctuating agricultural trends? How will farming skills be taught to urban workers? How will farmland be made available to city residents?

An extended work life is possible only when older workers themselves want to continue working. This is particularly relevant in the United States where, despite the elimination of mandatory retirement, the actual retirement age has steadily declined. In order to encourage older people to remain employed, it is necessary to create a social and cultural milieu in the workplace where they feel comfortable and needed. Such a milieu must benefit all employees, or younger workers will resent their senior colleagues. Realistic assessment of older workers' capabilities as well as appropriate adjustments in physical facilities, job assignments, and rewards that match productivity are recommended to create a positive work environment.

Eastern medicine preaches that man remains healthy when his elements are in harmony with nature. Farming is one of the practical ways of cultivating this harmony. The combination of factory or office careers with farming is certainly conducive to a healthy and productive life.

The Right to Choose an Extended Work Life

Douglas A. Fraser

The American industrial workers' quest for retirement began a little over 30 years ago. Then employers could not force a worker to retire because he or she had seniority. When we negotiated our first contract, employees resisted a pension, and the quid pro quo was that we would agree to compulsory retirement at age 68. I can recall those first meetings, when we advised these people—some of them in their 70s—that they had to retire. They had never even thought about it and were bitterly disappointed that they were forced out of the workplace. As time went on, it became a moot point. Now 95% of the 350,000 United Auto Workers (UAW) retirees retired voluntarily before the compulsory retirement age.

To have a successful retirement program, the workers must be able to retire with security and dignity. "Security" means the guarantee of a continued pension plan; "dignity" means being able to provide for oneself without help from anyone. Thus, for example, we have continued the same health care plan for retirees as they had when they were working.

Having talked to thousands of UAW retirees, I can safely say that they are a group who live fulfilling, satisfying, and happy lives. The important principle here is that everyone has to be allowed to grow his own way and follow his own course. There is

121

a great variety of what the retirees do in their retirement years; they scatter to the four winds.

It is ironic that we have come full circle now, and the employers who resisted a pension plan and then wanted compulsory retirement now try to negotiate disincentives for retirement because they do not want to lose the peoples' talents and contributions they make to the workplace. In addition, older workers have better attendance records than younger workers.

I feel sorry for the white-collar workforce that has no union. While they might receive a "golden handshake," they are also sometimes given a not-too-gentle push out the door. People are resentful, as they really don't want to retire and have a difficult time making the adjustment. There is an alternative to this: They have the right to decide whether to have a union in the workplace. If they decide against a union, they have to continue to let the company make all their decisions concerning working conditions, wages, and fringe benefits. I would hope that the employees would see the light.

The principal question before us is, "Can we extend the work life?" Obviously we can. I think that keeping people out of the workplace who want to be in it is an enormous waste, but that does not mean that we necessarily want to extend the work life of people in their present occupations. There is nothing thrilling about being on an assembly line for 30 or 35 years. People in such jobs have the right to make a voluntary, independent decision whether or not they want to stay beyond age 55 or 60. We have to maximize the options and the alternatives that people have as they approach retirement age, as well as after they have reached it.

Productivity and the Role of Public Policy

Jean K. Elder

In developing public policy, we must consider the obligation of maintaining the productivity of older people, as well as helping them remain self-sufficient in retirement years. My definition of productivity includes not only paid work, but also the contributions older persons can make as volunteers in their communities.

The Department of Health and Human Services is approaching the graying of America from a very positive perspective. The Administration on Aging, a component of the Office of Human Development Services, is already focusing much of its research and demonstration dollars upon the valuable contributions that can be made by older persons—as teachers, role models, volunteers and experts—through many demonstration grants and what we call intergenerational activities. We feel that the nine different intergenerational models we have funded differ and could be replicated in various other sites in the United States or other nations. They focus primarily on the employment of older persons in youth service activities, working with, for example, latchkey children, teenage mothers, and juvenile offenders. Obviously, we are seeking to benefit from a tremendous and largely untapped resource of skills and knowledge possessed by older Americans.

123

We are also emphasizing health care and health promotion. The Administration on Aging is working jointly with the Public Health Service, advocating improved health through outreach education, physical fitness, and individual training.

If we are to meet the challenges of the ever-shrinking support ratio, we need to remove some of the barriers, employer-biased or others, so that older workers are provided with work opportunities if they so desire. We are making a great effort to change the attitudes of employers who once were rather skeptical of hiring older persons, and we are studying the possibility of removing some of the financial or administrative burdens in the employment or retention of older workers. We guesstimate that currently a half-million older Americans would like to work but have not yet found the appropriate match for their skills.

One of my top priorities is the Family Giving Initiative, which holds great promise of helping to maintain vulnerable persons in noninstitutional settings. I believe as we look at productivity and work, we also need to look at employers as a real force in providing good caregiving models—not only for child care but also for elder care.

Another thing we have been trying diligently to do within the Administration on Aging is not only to talk philosophically about where we would like to take public policy, but also to do something about it. One way is through our research and development dollars. We have about 25 million dollars per fiscal year. About a third of this was spent this year on education and training such as career preparation in gerontology and in-service and information sharing. Another third was spent on funding demonstration model projects, which emphasize building systems and promoting linkages between the aging network and other organizations. The final third is being spent on health promotion activities.

My vision for the Office of Human Development Services focuses on productivity and the interdependencies of persons, whether they are children, youth, native Americans, the developmentally disabled, or aging Americans.

Equity for the Elderly—In and Out of the Work Force

Cyril F. Brickfield

The United States and Japan are both industrialized nations whose populations are aging; therein lies the problem.

In the United States we see two conflicting trends. On the one hand, we have early retirement. In 1960, 41% of those over 55 were still working or seeking employment; today, 25 years later, it has decreased to 30%. Although there are both work and social security benefits after age 65, there's an earnings limitation. It's really a form of mandatory retirement, because when you begin to earn more than $8,000 a year, you lose social security benefits, one dollar per every two, and pretty soon every three, that you earn.

There are too many corporations, unfortunately, that are inducing early retirement in their older employees through lump sum benefits. If you are 55 years old, you are given credit for another 5 years, so that your annualized benefits will be based on 60 years. We have a problem with that because this discriminates between those under 60 who are given a lump sum benefit and those between 60 and 65 or older. Often many of these lump sums turn out to be a disappointment, because, on an average, when stretched out, they bring about a lower annual benefit. Too, the people who take early retirement forego an average of perhaps 10 years of future earnings with that organization.

125

Finally, of course, there are the threats, expressed or implied. They say they will give an option for early retirement, but you must act within three or five months because that is the open application period. If you don't accept, they reserve the right to either relocate, reassign, or lay off. People get the word that they are no longer wanted, and that is a terrible feeling.

On the other hand, starting in the 1990s, fewer younger workers will be in the work force, probably dropping 25% to 1.1 million from approximately 3 million in 1960. Thus, there will be a need for older skilled workers.

In 1977 mandatory retirement was eliminated. But it is one thing to have a law on the books and another to make it work. The American Association of Retired Persons (AARP) is fighting mandatory retirement, informing workers of their rights. We are also engaging in litigation to fight age discrimination. Older workers have wage and competition problems. Industry feels a 54-year-old is not going anywhere, so he or she is not given any opportunity for advancement or retraining. In addition, few businesses have health care benefits for retirees. We have to bring about an education process, sensitizing businesses to the fact that the elderly are not only their customers but also their employees. We must tell them that 80% of all health care for the elderly is still delivered by the family, usually an oldest daughter. But now with women making up 51% of the work force, they often end up performing dual roles. So we ask industry to look at flex-time, for example, or perhaps to consider stipends for the older worker/caregiver. They should think about adult day care.

Women in the workplace face the same difficulties as minorities do, and they have pension problems because they have not been in the work force as long, so they do not earn the credits and benefits. In fact, in their entirety, private pensions are in a state of chaos. First of all, 50% of the work force today has no pension. That alone should be of great concern. And 75 to 80% of the other 50% have ineffective pensions that pay $55 or $150 or $300 a month—and what does that buy? That's why the AARP says, "Thank God for social security." It is there; it is universal.

But I think in the final analysis, if we are extending hands across the sea, that the elderly in Japan, just as the elderly in the

United States, need advocacy groups. They need to lobby for better working conditions. After all, Japan is a democratic country as is the United States, and we all know the old cliché, "The squeaky wheel gets the grease." The AARP has 26 million members—and there is power in numbers. We do not seek anything improper, but we certainly want to be heard. And we want the elderly to be heard. We are in a leadership role, and equity in the work force is paramount.

The Benefits of Extending the Work Life

F. Peter Libassi

The work life can be, should be, and, in fact, is beginning to be extended. Barriers, obstacles, and resistance are certainly there. Even public and private retirement and employment policies frequently work to frustrate such an extension. The elderly have conditioned themselves to think that their work life is limited once they reach 60, 62, or 65. Our business community is starting to see that some of the old rules ought to be discarded and some new, more flexible approaches to employment be considered. Certainly we have sufficient evidence that the work life can be extended and doing so will bring substantial benefits to older workers, business, society, and our economy. The one demographic fact that is driving the American business community to recognize this is that we're going to have fewer younger workers in the years ahead; thus, they're asking themselves how they can take advantage of the experience, skills, and abilities of older workers.

But we first have to ask why the trend toward early retirement continues. We have built a private pension system that, when combined with our public pension system, provides the American worker with the economic resources to retire. Also, from the worker's point of view, a certain status is attached to retiring early. Business and public sectors send conflicting signals to older workers. We eliminate mandatory retirement, but attitudes persist that older workers should move along and allow more room for younger and middle-aged workers to move up the career ladder. Our public programs were not designed to encourage continued employment, but rather to protect and encourage early retirement. I only wish Congress would seriously question whether the policy legislation now before it encourages workers to remain in the work force and employers to keep them there longer.

Flexible policies are being developed by employers, but the barriers and resistance to extending the work life remain serious. Some employers are beginning to respond to these opportunities out of necessity, realizing that retaining older workers actually makes good business sense because turnover and the recruiting and orienting of new workers are costly. They realize older workers have a stronger work ethic than younger workers and serve as positive models in the workplace. Certainly if their work life is extended, elderly people will be contributors to instead of recipients of the pension system and social security, they will contribute to the gross national product, paying taxes, buying goods, and spending money; in addition, expenditures for social welfare programs would be reduced.

There's ample evidence that the productive work life of older workers can be extended. Some 15 years ago Travelers began hiring back its retirees. We eliminated mandatory retirement in our offices nationwide before we were legally required to do so. We decided to change our pension plan so that our retirees could work six months a year without any loss of pension or health care benefits. Our retirees earn a reasonable salary, keep their pension, and, if they don't earn over $8,000, keep their social security. We introduced completely flexible, individually determined worker hours, giving tremendous flexibility not only to older workers, but also to the substantial number of female workers spending anywhere from 10 to 30 hours a week caring for an elderly dependent. We've established a retiree job bank whose sole purpose is to rehire our retirees for part-time or full-time temporary jobs. In fact, in 1985 we faced a major problem: We didn't have enough retirees to fill the job orders. Since we could not recruit enough of our own retirees, we opened the job bank to non-Travelers retirees. We still can't meet the supervisors' demands for retirees and are now launching a major newspaper advertising campaign in Hartford directed exclusively at retirees.

This program certainly meets a social and perhaps a national economic need and surely is in Travelers best interests. Our personnel department estimates we save 1 million dollars annually by directly hiring our retirees rather than using more costly programs through temporary employment agencies. Our supervisors say our retirees are excellent, thorough, and efficient workers.

The old adage "You can't teach an old dog new tricks" just does not hold true. Our retirees are in training programs with our newest employees of all ages without any problems. Too, problems of younger workers working with older workers just do not exist. Older workers often say that working with younger people makes them aware of today's issues and keeps them feeling young and a part of the world.

Corporations need to be concerned about the productivity of employees of all ages. We need employees who are enthusiastic about their work, have skills to contribute, like to work, and contribute to the company—and, I might say, to profits. So the answer is yes, we can extend the work life, and despite barriers to continued employment, the private sector certainly has a growing body of proof that older workers have important skills and enthusiasm to contribute to the company and to our economy. Certainly American business and older workers and our society stand much to gain if we would only let ourselves go and extend the work life.

Keeping Older People Productive   10

INTRODUCTION TO CHAPTER 10

Highlights of the symposium's panel discussion, moderated by Hugh Downs, contains the phrase "productive-age group." Takao Komine at first uses it in contrast to "the elderly," but the context shows us that "productive-age group" is as pliable as the latter phrase.

Society has defined the elderly apart from "productive-age group." Mr. Komine tells us that this definition is subject to change. The elderly population of tomorrow will differ from today's: A greater proportion will reach late life with great vigor and a desire to keep using it. The elderly themselves will redefine "productive-age group."

So will the economy—partly because (as Lou Harris sees for American society) there will be a labor shortage in the 1990s but also because the economy will need earners (a) to produce savings for investment and (b) to carry a burgeoning social security system. Thus, not 15 to 64, the current convention, but 15 to 70 or 75 will define "productive-age group," Mr. Komine notes. (And even these limits are open to question.)

To make the most of the productive potentials of older people, the United States and Japan will need to overcome obsolete attitudes. Daisaku Maeda refers to the practice of replacing older workers with less costly and (presumably) more efficient younger workers. This is a prescription for dependency, he notes. The practice raises the question of whether industrial policies (through automation and relative neglect of mass, low-income markets) actually contrive a labor surplus or job shortage, remedied in part by retiring older workers.

The discussants clearly see superannuation as a heavily socioeconomic construct having less to do with physical realities than commonly assumed. In less than six years, American history suggests, older workers were transformed from outcasts to desirables: The social security system was originated in 1935 during the Great Depression to release jobs for the young and to sustain elders who had lost employment. In World War II, because of labor shortages, U.S. older workers (and women workers, like Rosie the Riveter) were in great demand. No biological change requalified older persons (or women) for work—society needed them. The panel discussion approaches but only brushes the issue of guaranteed employment—or a right to work regardless of age—and its relevance to productive aging.

Why such an issue is neglected becomes clear, in part, from Lou Harris's observation. Elders harbor misconceptions of their age peers (no doubt echoing assumptions embedded in economic policies). Some 58% of elders think most older people are chronically ill but only 12% of the elderly see themselves as ill. Betty Friedan tells us that we are as much victims of a mystique about aging as about women: We are reluctant to see older people as capable.

Making use of these capabilities requires investment in training as well as opportunities for productive expression through paid employment and social or volunteer roles. As Tadashi Nakamura puts it, "Every possible means must be mobilized to guarantee work opportunities for the elderly." Trends, however, have gone in the opposite direction.

To waste this labor generates avoidable conflict between younger workers and (forced) retirees over limited social resources. For Amitai Etzioni, this tension has prompted injudicious calls for "intergenerational equity," basically reduction in social security benefits and, of course, taxes upon productive-age workers. In a tight economy with diminishing living standards, intergroup conflicts are hard to resolve. In any case, not allowing elders to work is socially divisive, he says. Meanwhile, Esther Peterson sees resources of the elderly drained away by commercial exploiters in the nursing home, insurance, and product fields.

The nature of political power is another focus of discussion. Richard Scammon says the American elderly are politically influential in every congressional district, and programs for them are seen as valuable by the young as well as the elderly. But Mr. Etzioni thinks elder political power is not often exercised. Mr. Harris finds older people using politics for regaining places in the mainstreams of life, not for a free ride. Mr. Nakamura says the conservatism of Japanese elders could turn radical if they can't get a fair deal.

How Japan and the United States adapt politically and economically to aging populations is of interest around the world. As Mr. Komine mentions, the two economies will account for one-third of world gross national product in the year 2000. If they can't handle the issues, who can?

PANEL DISCUSSION

LOU HARRIS: There are two misconceptions about aging. One, previously called the "rocking chair syndrome," has us believe that as people get older, they just rock and nod on a front porch. With that is whispered, "And you know, they're chronically ill." The saddest part is that 58% of those over 65 think that most of their age group is chronically ill, but we consistently find that only between 11 and 12% see *themselves* as being chronically ill. Thus, it is simply not true that the elderly are in a kind of dotage, that they're chronically ill and can't make it.

Another misconception is that a tremendous generational split exists. It is now difficult to mandate retirement. One reason for mandatory retirement was the notion of competition between the young and the old, that if the elderly went to work after 65, they would hold down all the jobs, and the young could never get a job. Our polls show that 78% of the young are in favor of abolishing mandatory retirement, even more than the elderly are (65%). As we continued polling, we discovered a tremendous love affair has been going on between the young and the old. They are two mutually supportive groups. Basically, then, there is no generational split.

DAISAKU MAEDA: The elderly's contribution through production was quiet apparent when we were an agricultural society. Most people were self-employed, and only the well-to-do could retire and be dependent upon their children. Most continued to work as long as their health permitted. Naturally, the elderly contributed to society in the same way as the younger generations—sometimes even more. In many cases, the knowledge, skills, and experiences they had accumulated throughout their lives were very useful. Even then, though, the proportion was small; most employed persons were under a strict mandatory retirement system, often with a low fixed age. Needless to say, the purpose of such a system was to replace older workers with less costly and more efficient younger ones.

In societies with predominantly secondary and tertiary industries and highly advanced technologies the knowledge and skills of older workers tend to quickly become obsolete. Mandatory retirement at a certain age is universally established. In other words, most older persons are not allowed to contribute to society through production. In addition, more and more married women are entering the labor market due to the automation of household jobs and an aspiration for economic independence resulting from higher education. Employers prefer to hire young and middle-aged women because their labor is cheaper and they learn new skills quicker.

Another unfavorable condition for older workers is competition with less industrialized countries. Due to the import of cheaper manufactured goods from such countries, job opportunities for unskilled or semiskilled laborers are decreasing. To make matters worse, industrialized economies are in a perpetually stagnant state, thus keeping a high unemployment rate.

However, even in industrialized and urbanized societies, older persons no longer expected to work as employees can continue to play other productive roles. For example, many aged painters, sculptors, musicians, and political and business leaders make indispensable contributions nationally and internationally.

Even the average older person can contribute to society. If self-employed, he can continue to contribute as young persons do. In farming or small independent retail shops, the elderly generally continue working as long as their health permits.

But how can all older retirees continue to contribute to society?

In Japan, the average mandatory retirement age is still considerably lower than that of other industrialized countries. Law stipulates that government employees retire at 60. In almost all large-scale business enterprises, retirement age can be as low as 56 to 58. Therefore, many retiring from governmental agencies or from large-scale firms seek jobs in related nongovernmental organizations or small firms, usually with much lower wages and social status. But many cannot find employment and become dependent on a pension. If the amount of public pension is large enough to live on, this is all right; however, present-day pensions often are not satisfactory. Thus, in Japan, job-finding services for retired older persons still play an important role in public social services.

The Japanese elderly do make other contributions to society. Contributors to the family are still significant, for over 60% aged 65 and over live with their adult children. As the International Plan of Action on Aging (adopted at the World Assembly on Aging held in Vienna, Austria, in May, 1982) stresses, the presence of grandparents "teaches an irreplaceable lesson" to children in the family. Since many young mothers work full time, the grandmother's role in child rearing and other domestic activity is indispensable. In three-generation households, more than 30% of older women are playing at least one of the following roles: caring for the family altar, cleaning the house, tending the house or the store while other family members are all out, washing dishes, preparing meals, washing clothes, and caring for grandchildren.

The elderly are also active in community volunteer activities. A past survey disclosed that approximately 40% of those aged 60 and over had some such experience, three times higher than that of young and middle-aged persons. Another survey revealed the most active volunteers are women in the 60 to 69 age group.

The Japanese government is also trying to promote activities of the elderly through various programs that find them opportunities to earn money to supplement the low public pensions, thereby enhancing their contribution to society and increasing their sense of fulfillment. The most comprehensive program currently supported by the government is the Senior Citizen Clubs, organized by older persons themselves. At present, there are approximately 100,000 clubs, with membership amounting to nearly half of the elderly population aged 60 and over.

Besides offering friendship and cultural/recreational activities, most clubs emphasize community volunteer activities such as friendly visits to homebound older persons and cleaning and beautifying public places. Some clubs engage in productive activities like fish breeding, mushroom cultivation, and making and selling traditional souvenirs. Others are interested in preserving traditional community culture through folk tales and music. In short, these clubs show that the elderly are still contributing members of society.

Under another program, the Ministry of Health and Welfare subsidizes 40 local governments for two years to provide places for the elderly to be engaged in contributive and/or creative activities, including woodworking, wood carving, ceramics, gardening, fish breeding, livestock raising, handicrafts, and weaving. Many similar programs are run by local governments.

The Ministry of Health and Welfare also operates 148 urban centers for the utilization of the elderly's abilities, finding jobs for those who want to earn money through employment. As an employment office for the elderly, the Center plays an important role in teaching various firms and the community as a whole that the elderly can contribute to society through various jobs.

The Ministry of Labor sponsors the Silver Manpower Center, an agency organized and run by a group of retired persons wanting to continue to work for additional income, thereby contributing to both family and society. These workers are not employed by the Center nor by the job providers, but are self-employed under contract with the Center and fill part-time positions provided by local governments, firms, and sometimes citizens of the community. Some Centers run their own business ventures to provide jobs for members. In addition to 260 nationally supported centers, local governments have established similar agencies.

The Ministry of Agriculture, Forestry, and Fishery has a number of subsidiary programs promoting various activities for the elderly. With the modernization of agricultural production, needed manpower has been significantly reduced, and many younger people have gone to urban areas to find jobs. Thus, middle-aged and younger persons who remain in rural areas are usually fully occupied with farm work and have little time for community activities not directly related to production. With the shortage of manpower, lighter farm labor often is carried out by persons over 70.

Recognizing this, the Ministry provides local governments or agricultural cooperatives a special grant or loan to assist a group of the elderly who want to continue to work and thereby contribute to the community. These grants or loans may be used to obtain needed facilities for collaborative agricultural activities, such as a farm, a ranch, a factory, a machine, or a building. Besides expenditures for capital formation, some programs allow money to be used for training and meetings. One well-known program for the rural elderly supports cow breeding by the elderly themselves. This program subsidizes local governments or agricultural cooperatives in loaning calves to the rural elderly, who breed them and repay the loan after selling them at the market.

Finally, a conflict exists between contribution to society and pursuit of self-realization. One significant difference between less and more industrial societies is that in the latter, owing to the development of income maintenance programs, older persons are more economically independent. They can choose to either contribute to the family and community or pursue self-realization, as many younger people do.

People sometimes talk about the younger generation or society itself exploiting the elderly by making them feel compelled to do things for their families or society without remuneration. Even in a family the exploitation of the elderly can occur. For example, a married daughter frequently asks her mother to take care of her children while she pursues a hobby, yet the mother herself wants to attend regular adult education classes. There is no problem if the mother willingly accepts this task, but if, for some reason or other, she feels that she is compelled to do so, this may be regarded as a type of exploitation. The elderly may also be exploited socially if they feel they are being compelled by society to do something for inadequate remuneration. Thus, when considering the elderly's contributions, we should take into account their right to pursue their own self-realization.

Retired persons in highly aged societies have important roles to play. It is estimated that by the middle of the next century, one-fifth to even one-fourth of the population in industrialized countries will be aged 65 and over. Senior citizens who are only interested in self-realization and who pay little attention to their potential contributions to family, community, and society will antagonize the rest of the population. Thus, in addition to constructing better social security, health care, and social service programs, we must prepare for the coming of an aged society in this respect as well.

BETTY FRIEDAN: About 25 years ago I was writing *The Feminine Mystique,* which dealt with a subtle and not so subtle distorted image of women in 20th century America that completely denied their personhood. Women were defined then by the mass media and textbooks only in terms of their relation to men: wife, mother, sex object, server of physical needs. A woman never was seen as a person, defining herself by her own actions in society. As a result, women were seen and saw themselves not as people.

I called it "the problem that has no name." A woman felt guilty because she didn't get the kitchen sink pure white or her husband's shirts ironed right. But there were no words for the problem of a woman herself in terms of her own existence in society.

She was a freak and she was alone if she didn't fit the image of the happy, fulfilled housewife.

What I see today is an "age mystique," almost more deadly than the feminine mystique in the denial of the personhood of people over 60, over 70, over 80, over 90. I see the necessity to break through this denial of age and the mystique that defines age only in terms of deterioration from youth—and male youth at that. Age is taken seriously only in one respect: You can sell people billions of dollars of products to try to pretend they are young. However, I am not 66 years *young;* I am 66 years *old* and going on to a new development in my own life, taking on new questions and new problems with maybe even more spunk and vigor than I ever had. But my reality is completely denied, for there is reluctance to see older people as productive.

Where is there a readiness of society to break through this denial, to look at the personhood, the strengths that have no names, of people over 50, 60, 70, 80—women and men—and see what might emerge, to look at age as a new gift of human development and human potential? There are two ways we now take: one is to sell more things to the elderly to help them pretend they are young; the other is to treat them as objects of our compassionate, tolerant care.

It is not going to work much longer. The elderly are going to stimulate the revolution that opens and changes society, giving it new music. They are not going to be the problem but rather the revolution that changes the definitions and the values. This revolution will be just as life affirming and life opening as the Women's Movement and the Youth Movement and the Black Civil Rights Movement. Women are going to lead this revolution, for they are living eight years longer than men.

We have been educated by the Women's Movement. We have already changed our lives and society. We don't buy any of these miserable, compassionate definitions. We still continue to define ourselves. We will not go gently into the good night but will bring the country into a new day.

AMITAI ETZIONI: The one thing we do not need, the one thing that would make our lives more productive if we could decide to do without it, is a deliberate attempt to create a war between the generations. It doesn't exist and there is no reason to seek it. I am saddened that the organization Americans for Generational Equity (AGE) was created with the argument that the elderly are taking too many resources, leaving not enough for the young, and that we have to find ways of cutting back on what they are taking from us.

The effort to steer the intergenerational fight is based on very simple misconceptions about how the economy works. First is the notion (and defense contractors are worried about this) that if social services are increased, not enough money will be left for additional weapons. We don't have a zero-sum game here, that if you give something to one, you have to take it from the other. We simply have to recognize that the economy is currently sluggish. What we need is an economy that grows more. Instead of accepting a sluggish economy, we should be fighting and worrying about one that competes and grows productively.

Second is the notion that the world is divided only into social services and defense and there are no more slices. We're spending $2 billion a year on plastic surgery, some of which is very important, but some of it is cosmetic—tucks and lifts. And if we are down to the question of either buying guns or allowing our senior citizens to retire, maybe we could first cut some of that $2 billion before we come to the harsh, unreal choices.

One of the worst scare tactics that AGE promotes is the suggestion that because of the increase in the older population, young workers will have to pay 42% of their payroll into Social Security, and by the time they retire, nothing will be left for them. This is absolutely unfounded. There is just no way that 42% of the payroll will be dedicated to Social Security. The truth is that at the moment Social Security is running a hefty surplus, which is used to reduce the deficit created by defense spending. If anybody is really concerned about the future of Social Security, let's remove it from the budget completely and let defense pay for itself; let's stop using it to cover other deficits. In effect, by the year 2000, Social Security surpluses may run somewhere around a trillion dollars.

We are one family. We need one another. We need more intergenerational support. We need more grandparents helping the
youngsters and the youngsters helping the grandparents. The
saddest part of this attack on the generations is that it's driving
wedges into the family when the last thing the family needs is
more people pulling it down.

TADASHI NAKAMURA: Over the past 25 years, Japan has con-
centrated on creating or maintaining employment opportunities
for the elderly. A social consensus was gradually formulated that
(1) the extension of the retirement age is a must, with the target
age of 60; (2) the need to guarantee work opportunities for those
between 60 and 65 must be met by extending the employment
and/or rehiring system, as well as the retirement age; and (3) the
opportunity to participate in social activities by those over 65
should be assured. By 1986, two-thirds of our enterprises had
changed or were planning to change the retirement age from 55
to 60 and older.

Over the last 15 years, the elderly work force has grown by 3
million, 60% aged 55 to 59. Within the next 15 years, it will increase by another 4 million, with 30% aged 60 to 65 and 40% 65
and older. Thus, the elderly will increase from the present one-
sixth to one-fourth of the total work force.

In this connection, it is important to note four possibilities.
First, although within the past 15 years the younger labor force
has dropped by 4 million, it is anticipated to grow by 2 million
within the next 15 years as the children of the baby boomers
enter it, implying that employers will rely more on younger
rather than older generations to fill vacancies. Second, female
labor force participation will continue to grow both in volume
and speed, though to a lesser degree than over the last decade.
Women will compete with the elderly in the labor market by
seeking employment in tertiary industries and choosing part-
time jobs. Third, faced with an uncertain exchange rate, a pressure of protectionism in world trade, and a possible low growth
in the world economy, Japanese employers are beginning to
feel that redundancy in their enterprise is unbearable and

adjustment of employment is unavoidable. Fourth, expanding
the pension system will never occur because of a government
budget deficit and upsurge of the elderly population. Thus, the
elderly's future may not be dark, but it is gray.

In light of this, every possible means must be mobilized to
guarantee work opportunities for the elderly so that their willingness to participate in social activities is satisfied, thus contributing to economic growth, social stability, and well-being. In
this connection, three major instruments must be mentioned: (1)
life-long education and training enabling workers to both adapt
to changing job content and also participate positively in social
activities in their later working lives; (2) a shorter working day
so that such training can be pursued and wider part-time opportunities can be created for the elderly; and (3) a life-long health
plan for workers.

Throughout history, mankind has shown its sincere desire to
live longer. When this desire becomes a reality, will we then
view it as a tragedy? I cannot accept that.

RICHARD SCAMMON: Basically, American politics features a
weak party system and a concentration on interests. Real policy
decisions are not made by political parties with ideological or
even pragmatic views. They are made by coalitions of interests,
by people who make decisions based upon the varied interests
they represent. Thus, in a democratic system like ours, policy
decisions depend largely on pure numbers.

The aged, like blacks, women, and Hispanics, have influence
because they have votes, and their influence on Congressional
members to enact legislation that helps older citizens is increasing measurably. Unlike farmers or blacks, the aged are pretty
well distributed around the country. Every Congressional district has a substantial number of older citizens interested in such
problems as retirement age, medical attention, and Social Security. The elderly's potential influence on the political system is
great, more so because, for example, unlike blacks, the majority
is not easily identifiable as Republican or Democrat. Their numbers in both parties are substantial, resulting in their ability to
defend and advance their interests substantially.

Additionally, many younger people join in these interests, for should elderly support programs end, their caretaking problems would increase measurably. One major reason for the development and increase of Social Security benefits was its appeal not to older voters but younger voters who didn't have to concern themselves as much as they might have otherwise with the problems of aging parents.

Under these circumstances, I cannot look at the future without a good deal of optimism that my vote and the vote of many others in my age group will have additional influence, and if one may be politically pragmatic, additional threat. Nothing makes a Congressman tune his ear than lots of votes.

TAKAO KOMINE: A 1982 report released by the Economic Planning Agency, *Japan in the Year 2000*, helps explain how to cope with an aging society. It should be fully possible for us to handle the aging society if we grasp the problems correctly and make appropriate responses. In addition, the problems should be looked at in an international framework. Japan and the United States will account for one-third of the total world gross national product in 2000. As we deal with our aging societies, the most important question is how to keep our economic vitality—how to raise and maintain productivity. If lost, it will harm the development of world economy.

The average age of Japan's population is rising rapidly. Those aged 65 or over comprised 10.3% of the total population in 1985; it will be 16.3% in 2000 and 23.6% in 2020. The percentage of older people in Japan will be the highest in the world, for Japan has the longest life expectancy and has witnessed a sharp drop in the birth rate since 1973. Its population is aging faster than that of other nations. For instance, in European nations, it took between 45 and 135 years for the proportion of people 65 or over to rise from 7% to 14%; in Japan, it took only 26 years.

After the year 2000, the number of young people will stabilize, while the number of those aged 65 or over will continue to swell. As a result, the percentage of productive-age persons in the population will start to fall off sharply, reaching 61.5% in 2020. From the economic standpoint, this decline means that the people who are engaged in productive activity must produce more and devote more of their income to supporting the elderly.

This burden will affect working morale. Here, the social security system will play an important role. Though the Japanese social security system is regarded as lagging behind those of other industrial nations, it is quite similar to that of the United States and European countries. At present, its expenditures and contributions are not large compared with these nations because Japan's population is still relatively young. Contributors still greatly outnumber recipients. As society ages, it is anticipated that the scale of pension payments—and thus the burden on working people—will greatly expand.

Additionally, the overall savings rate will fall by 2 to 3% between 1980 and 2000. Individual households normally save money while their family members are engaged in productive activity and live on these savings after retirement. If the pattern of saving in individual households remains unchanged, a bigger share of older people in the total population will mean a lower savings rate.

To cope with such economic problems, we need to take various measures, the most important of which is to create employment opportunities for older people. Employment for retirees is needed not only because it provides income, but also because it will allow the elderly to continue to use their experience and feel useful. Also, from the macroeconomic standpoint, it will lessen the burden on the productive-age generation. To make the labor market more open to the elderly, educational and training opportunities must be provided; additionally, forms of employment geared to the aged's physical capacities and desire to work will also be needed.

According to the present international definition, people aged 65 or over belong to the aged group, and people aged 15 to 64 belong to the productive-age group. But a 65-year-old in the 21st century will be different from today's 65-year-old. If we can succeed in making older people healthier and delaying the physical and mental weakening processes by 5 or 10 years, we can redefine the aged group as those 70 or 75 years or over and the productive-age group as those 15 to 69 or 74. This will give us a better perspective for dealing with the aging society in the 21st century.

ESTHER PETERSON: The elderly are the most vulnerable group now in the marketplace. People are willing to play on their fears, desires, and hopes. We need to examine the hidden persuaders of the marketplace busily moving into this new territory.

Now there are two sides to the marketplace. One supplies all kinds of splendid goods and services, but the down side exploits. Why? I think much is due to the elderly's loneliness, their hope for cures, and their desire for economic help.

The elderly are exploited by nursing home abuse. I think that health quackery is most serious. Then there is the exploitation by the cosmetics industry with its creams for sagging skin and other products to make us look right and smell nice. Mail fraud is another big one—"Earn $600 at home," and you usually find this means stuffing envelopes. Investment scams in real estate are paramount today. And we are always told we need more insurance. Much of this comes in beautiful envelopes, appearing to be government sponsored, but is really just a come-on used again to get a hold on the people. A lot of these are just dishonest, and we do not catch up with them. I'm concerned about that.

The elderly fall for a lot of this, and they end up in a vicious circle. They spend their money; they get sick and must use their resources more quickly; with their resources gone, they become discouraged and more sick; and the cycle continues.

But it does not have to be that way. I'm the eternal optimist. I have lived a long time and have seen the progress that has been made. If all of us working together obtain the forces needed to educate and protect the consumer, we can then move on into other areas such as policy and nourishment to make the promise of productive aging a reality.

HUGH DOWNS: What we have heard thus far outlines the problems we face and hints at remedies—some a little surprising. The hidden "facts" have intrigued me most. For example, it is a myth that the generations do not like each other. In fact, a poll indicated that Americans respect Japan most for its attitude

toward and treatment of its elders. Thus, we want to do right by
our elders, but why aren't we doing it? I suspect that inertia has
much to do with it. The question I want to ask now is, as we move
into the era of productive aging, are we going to have effective
and humane policies? Is it realistic to suppose we will not suffer
terrible dislocation when this occurs and find we are not ready?

PETERSON: I agree with Mr. Scammon that we must take advantage of our political power. I am seeing groups getting together on a common denominator of belief, and the power is
tremendous. I think we can influence with political power.

HARRIS: I disagree. Those 65 and older do have a 2½ times
better chance of voting on election day than those under 25, and
heaven knows, if the elderly did not have political clout, they
would be nowhere. But I would suggest from studies we have
done that the elderly want to be the first group ever to use its
political power not to gain benefits to the exception of other
population groups, but instead to say: "Please let us be part of
the mainstream of the human race. Don't pity us. Let us earn our
way and contribute in a mainstream way." That is why they will
use their political power.

ETZIONI: It is not correct to view any group as simply an interest group out to get as much of the total as it can. Yes, there are
interest groups, but there are many more Americans, old and
young, who have combined their self-interest with interest in the
common good. If the elderly had this tremendous political clout
they are alleged to have, we would long ago have had the elemen-
tary health insurance which exists in all other industrialized
societies; we would not have to dump them into nursing homes;
we would not cut back on Medicare; we would not thin out
Social Security.

    Yes, there are interest groups. They are part of a pluralistic
democratic society. But they fight with one hand tied behind
their backs, using the other hand to worry about a decent society
for all of us. The last thing we should do is promote a cynical
view of society and move people away from the common interest

toward self-interest. Nor should we view Congress simply as a money exchanger to whom all the interest groups come and get their checks cashed. If there is no other concern here in these halls for the country, for the future, than paying off various constituencies, we will not be fully prepared for the future. We will never do all we can and should do.

But one of the most productive things happening that will continue happening is doing away with this figure 65 we are stuck on. Maybe it would help if we were reminded of where it came from. It is about 148 years old, concocted by Bismarck in his fight with the Social Democrats. Since they wanted social services, he said everybody above 65—which then was very few—could get all they wanted. It was his trick. But today we have a fantastic life expectancy, and the figure is ridiculous. All we have to do is abolish it. We need to stop treating people as categories and allow them to retire when they want rather than at a fixed point.

I know nine people who work in the underground economy so that they will not lose Social Security benefits. Not allowing older Americans to work without penalty decreases Treasury revenues and creates a separate class of people—one that works without fringe benefits in order to augment Social Security income. Removing the penalty would result in an enormous statistical change. Although on the records only 11% of Americans over 65 work, I would bet at least another 11 to 22% work off the record. Consequently, if we change our definitions and our concepts, we will be much more prepared to face our joint future.

NAKAMURA: In Japan the elderly are generally thought of as belonging to conservative groups, while those younger belong to progressive or liberal groups. Should the elderly's desires not be met and they thus join the progressive or revolutionary groups, society's balance would be upset.

DOWNS: That is an interesting point, but that doesn't eliminate the need to be active.

PETERSON: We must not overlook the people over 65 who are volunteering.

DOWNS: The Women's Movement had to start from scratch, more or less. It didn't have the aging population's benefits in terms of increasing numbers and an organization that's been going on for quite some time. Will it be easier for the movement to help older people than it was for the Women's Movement to help women?

FRIEDAN: Women were and are 52% of the population. The Women's Movement began with winning the vote. For a century women battled for their rights, but because it had been a battle for equality in male terms, the dreams got buried. Our feminine mystique almost denied or prevented any political activity, so we had to invent the wheel all over again. The consciousness was critical, for any revolution begins in consciousness. Such consciousness will increase as we move toward the end of the century when those of my generation, having new vital years of life, are joined by the post–World War II baby boomers who will have a basic revolutionary effect on the values of society, just as the Women's Movement has had. As we come to new terms with personhood, not trying to pretend we are young but defining our maturity and asserting our wisdom and values, the whole political picture might change.

DOWNS: I often think of something Harvey Wheeler said: The time will come when it will be prestigious to be old and young people will pretend to be older. Consequently, cosmetics companies will bring out new products to help young people look older.

ETZIONI: It's believed more wealth is transferred from the young to the old when, in fact, for every dollar those under 65 give to those over 65, those over 65 given two dollars in return. Many children return home after the second divorce or the third job to live with older parents.

HARRIS: Only 6% of those 65 and over work, but literally 68% say they would like to work—and it is incredible that 30% of all those 65 and older are living alone; 64% live with a spouse; 16% live with their children or friends. These 16% living with others don't like it, but those living with spouses do. Of those living alone, 81% are widowed and 33% are 80 years or older. Their average income, $5,100, is far below the poverty line; 48% say they suffer from depression; 38% are afraid to let people into their homes; 13% sometimes go without medical help because they can't afford it. But many still say they would rather live alone. Why? They want to be independent, to earn their own way, and they will do anything to do it.

When we have a big labor shortage in the 1990s and have to turn to the elderly as one of our labor source pools, we will find they are ripe and ready to work. We are a paper-pushing society and not a mule-hauling one any longer. Older people can do the job.

DOWNS: We welcome any questions the audience may have for a specific panelist. In the meantime, I would like to follow up on something that was said earlier about changing our social attitudes. When I was in Nepal, I found it was quite polite to be asked how old you are. If you answer apologetically, "I'm only 50," the proper, polite response is, "Well, that's all right. You're getting there." They revere age. Yet, when we say, "Gee, you don't look that old," it is supposed to be a compliment. Will that turn around in time? Will we really have a healthier attitude toward a full life expectancy?

QUESTIONER: Do you see any analogy to the general phenomenon of scapegoating in our history and in other countries?

ETZIONI: There is a prejudice against the old, and prejudice has many roots. One is scapegoating. We are moving into a very tight economic environment. Our standard of living will not grow at the same pace as it did in previous generations, and maybe it has to be cut, at least for a transition period. Unfortunately, when society faces a tightening economy, conflicts among all groups become more difficult to deal with. In a growing economy, you can compensate and ease the pain by giving to a growing group that had been disadvantaged and don't have to worry about taking away from anybody. In a tightening environment, not only can't you give to everybody, but you have to start taking away from others in order to survive. Until we learn again to earn our keep and not live on foreign aid, we will have those pressures, and they will be reflected in prejudice.

HARRIS: In answer to your question, I don't think people are prone to be older-people bashers, making scapegoats of them. The most criminal thing that can be done to someone older is to ignore him and put him away. We find older people hate these "older people cities," these "ghettoized" places. The turnover rate is huge. Why? Because they say, "Good God, all you want us to do is wake up every morning to hear the clanging of the ambulance bell." They can't stand being pitied and ignored; what they want above all else is to be a part of the human race, not invisible.

QUESTIONER: What specific industries or businesses does the panel see as being most profoundly affected or that would benefit the most from the demographic changes and projections, particularly the aging of the baby boom generation?

ETZIONI: Before anybody generates new business based on those statistical profiles, they should take into account that the statistics assume no immigration, or certainly no illegal immigration. We are really not sure of its size, its age composition, or its change due to the new laws. Statistics are inaccurate because immigration has to be younger than average.

HARRIS: The Conference Board found 62% of all consumption dollars are spent by people 50 and over. American industry better wake up and realize where the money really is.

DOWNS: Why the lag? The public is quite astute. We know certain things, yet we don't close the gap.

FRIEDAN: The lag can be explained somewhat by what I call the "age mystique." The obsession with youth has made us dye our hair and have our faces lifted. This simply doesn't work anymore. Because there is such a denial of reality, there is no legislation dealing with real needs.

HARRIS: The only explanation I can give is it takes people about 20 years to claw their way to the top. They've worked so hard at it, but when they get there, they're 20 years out of date.

QUESTIONER: Just as I advocate that we should not accept loss of our memory and loss of our vital functions, I also do not apologize for not wanting to lose my looks as well. I think that self-esteem is very much associated with how we look, and it should be an individual choice as to how we look as we age. It is a right. I believe the biology of aging is such that one day, just as the arteries will not be so fragile, so, too, the skin will not sag so much. I think we should not accept that our faces change with age.

DOWNS: I wonder if there is a key to changing more quickly a cultural outlook that appears sluggish. Arthur Clarke told me once that missionaries had attempted for generations to get very primitive societies to abandon the practice of putting a bone through the central cartilage of the nose. It was not sinful in their minds, but to the missionaries it was defacing. They thought they could pressure tribe members out of it, but there was nothing they could do until the Polaroid camera was introduced. They then discovered a person could not focus a Polaroid camera with a bone in his nose. In about a year, the whole practice disappeared. Arthur said what we need is the moral equivalent of the Polaroid camera.

QUESTIONER: I am concerned about a report issued by the Institute of Medicine about a year ago that addressed productive roles in an aging society. It questioned whether it was realistic to expect volunteer contributions from the elderly segments of the population. Do we need to stick with the conventional, traditional definition, understanding that volunteerism means no compensation? It seems that perhaps volunteerism needs to be redefined so that there can be various forms of compensation, although I would wonder, too, about the appropriateness of even having some monetary form of compensation. We're beginning to hear some things about

"stipend volunteers," or subsidizing the volunteerism with payment for certain expenses that come along with it, or completely nonmonetary involvement by a person giving hours or
days or weeks and having that put into an account as a credit
against which he or anyone he designates could then draw on
for benefits equivalent to the input he had provided. I wonder
whether the panel has views on this as to where we go with
volunteerism, particularly by the elderly.

PETERSON: I think there are all kinds of service opportunities
for people. I would rather see people work at day care centers
than shoveling hamburgers in a fast-food restaurant. We need
jobs that have dignity, ones that do not take jobs away from
people who have to work early in life. The possibilities are limit-
less, and certainly there could be a stipend to cover expenses. I
think that is one of the greatest areas to explore.

QUESTIONER: I want to compliment Mr. Harris on his plea that
older people be considered part of the total society. It seems
when a person gets to be 65 and is not working, he has lost a vote,
a membership, the potential for doing something so that people
on the whole do not seem to give him credit for the maturity he
had when he was 64. One thing that you might be interested in,
though, is a tremendous amount of our social life comes from
work.

   I'd like to ask Ms. Peterson if she thinks we should have another Blue Sky Law to protect older people. Should we educate
them so that we keep a disproportionate number from getting
defrauded?

PETERSON: There are a number of things we could do. We
could see that the laws on the books are enforced, but a tremendous amount of education must take place with it.

QUESTIONER: Something still rings false to me about the intergenerational equity issue. It reminds me of the playground days
when one group of boys would urge another group of boys to
fight, provoking an argument. Even the word "equity" bothers

me, because it rings of an issue of finance, not one of fairness. I would rather discuss intergenerational fairness. It almost begins to look as if we older people are being accused of being unfair to the young. But as an older parent, I want a better education and health care system for my children than I had, and I would hope they would not be as patient as we were.

Response from Government

11

INTRODUCTION TO CHAPTER 11

In this chapter, as well as throughout the entire symposium, voices of policymakers mingled with those of scientists, pointing up mutual needs and collaborative potentials of science and policy. Gathered in this section are the remarks of members of Congress, providing as stimulating a set of outlooks in the realm of policy as that found in the realm of science. Also noteworthy is that the members of Congress broke off from legislative work to make their comments. What they were working on, in many instances, bore on productive-aging issues, including expansion of health care, social services, and job promotion activities for older persons. Thus, many conference issues had immediate relevance to the legislators. And they said so.

To cite a few contributions, Senator John Glenn embraced social planning and personal planning for productive aging. Senator Orrin Hatch, among others, sees the potential contribution of biomedical research to effective treatment and prevention of disabilities that limit productivity. Representative Claude Pepper saw later-life productivity as involving policies to promote health and stimulating jobs. Representative Edward Roybal emphasizes the synergism of employment policy and long-term care policy.

The shortage of geriatrics-trained health care professionals is noted by Senator James Sasser, fresh from introducing legislation on that subject.

The global nature of productive-aging issues is the theme sounded by Senator Larry Pressler, while Representative Patricia Saiki—herself of Japanese descent—points to biomedical research opportunities inherent in parallel studies of Japanese and Japanese-American populations. As Senator Spark Matsunaga, also an American of Japanese ancestry, puts it: "Collaborative efforts between the United States and Japan can only benefit both of our countries."

Cultural Studies Denote Biomedical Research Opportunities

Patricia Saiki

Because of my affinity with both Japan and America, I find the sharing of information and research between our two countries most encouraging. Hawaii's large Japanese-American population provides the perfect model for comparing the health, welfare, changes in customs, attitudes, and educational patterns of the Japanese in Hawaii compared with the Japanese in Japan.

Over the years I have been privileged to work on various research committees aligned with Hawaiian hospitals. I served for 15 years as a member of the St. Francis Hospital research committee. My husband, a physician also very interested in aging, has been on various committees of the board of Cortini Hospital, which specializes in the aged.

The similarities and differences between the aging populations of Japan and the United States have been covered over the many exhaustive hours you have spent exchanging your ideas. But it is interesting to note that Japan's over-65 population is 10.2% of its total population; in the United States, it is 11.5%. Thus, our over-65 populations are pretty close percentage-wise. Similarly, our interests and concerns are very much alike. As we expect our people to live even longer, we have to look at their needs and their concerns. The House of Representatives Select Committee on Aging is concentrating on many areas, and the

House itself is going to be coming forward with legislation that will have a further impact on the retirement age. We're going to be looking at various issues affecting catastrophic health care and affordable housing.

Research is absolutely necessary. The research committee at St. Francis Hospital authorized quite a few studies comparing Japanese-Americans with Japanese in Japan, specifically in the area of cancer, because we wanted to look at how diet, living conditions, and even the weather affect the individual's health and welfare. We learned from a study conducted by the University of Hawaii Medical Center, comparing the health of Japanese people in Japan and those who immigrated to Hawaii, that the Japanese-Americans living in Hawaii are one-third less likely to contract stomach cancer than are Japanese living in Japan. When you come out with that kind of data, you then have to search further to learn why. It seems the finding was largely attributed to the high fruit and vegetable content in the diet of the Japanese-Americans in Hawaii compared with the high-salt, cured, and pickled products consumed in Japan. There are numerous other studies available at the University of Hawaii, Cortini Hospital, and St. Francis Hospital if you want to get to the specifics of comparing Japanese-Americans and Japanese in Japan. Thus, research is absolutely critical in order to look toward and prepare for the future.

There is one more area where we have to develop a greater understanding and appreciation: the cultural attitudes and differences that have an impact on the aged. (Maybe having a Japanese background allows me to understand and appreciate this a lot more than some of my colleagues.) Within the Japanese culture, there is great respect for the older citizen. You learn very early as a child that you must respect your elders. The family unit is very tight. We are finding, of course, that in today's society, with housing needs being so prevalent, families are pulled apart; the older parent sometimes has to be left behind or live in a separate housing unit. This is beginning to tear the fabric of Japanese society. But it becomes even more difficult and traumatic when it is a Japanese parent who is struck with a catastrophic illness and is in need of long-term care. Then, unless we change the law, we are in a situation where we must make those families go destitute before we can give them the care that they really need. This is really affecting the Japanese-American population, especially in Hawaii, where it's a choice between sacrificing their children's education or the care of their mother or father.

As Japan and the United States work on these challenges, they cannot ignore the cultural changes that are occurring in our two countries as our populations get older.

The Need for Geriatrics-Trained Health Care Professionals

James Sasser

We share a number of assets and a number of problems in common with our Japanese friends. One problem—that hopefully can be turned into an asset—is that of an aging population.

I like the emphasis on the term "productive aging." From a public policy standpoint, Congress has dealt with the elderly as a potential burden on society. That's unfortunate and a misnomer, for they really are potential assets. If we can improve the quality of lives of our elderly citizens, we stand to be a richer nation for it.

The graying of America promises to be one of the most serious health care challenges in the years ahead, and when we look at the statistics and see the percentage of our population that's going to fall into the very-old category (85 and above) within the next 20 years, we quickly realize that we must address the problems of an aging population. Yet this nation's medical community remains largely unprepared to meet this challenge.

The problem is really very simple. Relatively speaking, we have very few physicians who are adequately trained to deal with the unique and chronic and complex ailments that strike the elderly. The Institute of Medicine has issued a report that reveals just how few American physicians there are with experience in geriatrics. Of the 450,000 practicing physicians in the United States, only

450—one in every thousand—have completed a postgraduate fellowship program in geriatrics. The Institute points out that we must double our current yearly output of geriatricians; the projected need is at least 2,100 geriatricians by the year 2000.

It's encouraging to note that steps have been taken recently to improve geriatric training here in our country, but these efforts are falling far short of what is needed. For example, in the current academic year, only three geriatricians are in advanced training in all of the United States.

Geriatricians have been largely ignored because this field is perceived by most in the medical community as not being very glamorous. American medicine has always focused on mass cures to dramatic, acute illnesses, and that's understandable. But there rarely are fast cures for the chronic ailments that afflict our elderly population. In fact, their conditions often defy a doctor's natural desire to make it all better in a hurry. As a result, physicians have a natural tendency to lose interest in elderly patients because the results are so slow in coming. They are often seen as hopeless cases, even when they may greatly benefit from medicine. I'm sure we all have heard the story of the 92-year-old man who went to the doctor complaining of a pain in his left leg. The doctor listened and finally declared, "Well, Sam, for Pete's sake, what do you expect at the age of 92?" Sam replied, "Well, Doctor, look at my right leg. It's also 92 and it's not hurting. Now explain that." Thus, doctors and all medical personnel must be taught that the chronic ailments of the elderly are not always hopeless conditions. Their treatment may require more time, more attention, and more patience, but positive results can be achieved and may, indeed, be spectacular.

We must act convincingly to correct our past neglect of this very vital and important area of medicine. We simply must act now, as we see our population continue to age and to age rapidly. That's why I introduced legislation that offers hope of improved medical care for our senior citizens. Based on the recommendation of the Institute of Medicine's upcoming report on geriatric medicine, it authorizes the establishment of Centers of Excellence in Geriatric Research and Training in 10 medical schools across the country that will develop critically needed academic leaders in the whole field of geriatrics. Once we have the academics, our medical schools will be able to train adequate numbers of practicing physicians in other health professions to care for the rapidly increasing numbers of older Americans.

Three years ago, while traveling in the Soviet Union with Senator Clayborne Pell, who has a profound interest in the problems of the aging, we went down into the Soviet Republic of Georgia where they say some people live considerably beyond 100 years. We met some of those old people, and they were living very happy and productive lives. But I was struck by the fact that the Soviet government had a large team of physicians there, trying to determine why these people were living to such old ages—more important, why they were living to such old ages in such good health. I then realized that the United States has no comparable interest nor comparable study of its own very old citizens.

This year Congress has the opportunity to expand our senior citizens' access to health care and to get deeper into the study of their health problems. We need to offer them more protection against catastrophic illness. Congress is starting to focus on that. They are tentative steps, to be sure, but, as the old Chinese proverb goes, a journey of 1,000 miles begins with the first step; I think this year Congress is beginning to take the first halting steps. That's good news for our senior citizens.

But as we expand our older Americans' access to health care, we should be equally committed to securing their access to high-quality medical care. We have pediatricians who specialize in caring for our children, but our seniors should also have access to physicians who are just as interested and just as knowledgeable about their special health care needs. If we are to offer high-quality health care to our aging population in the decades ahead, we must improve our nation's academic training and research in the field of geriatrics.

The Social and Economic Challenges of an Aging Society

Edward Roybal

Few issues carry as many promising dimensions as productive aging. For older Americans, it promises continued mental, physical, and economic well-being. For employers, it promises a stable work force over longer periods of time. For all generations, it promises economic security. Tremendous scientific and technological advances are allowing older persons to live longer and stay productive; however, such advances also produce potentially difficult social and economic challenges for our nations.

One challenge is the need for new employment policies that accommodate older workers. A second challenge is developing the types of services employees need to take care of dependent relatives, without themselves having to leave work. Increasingly, these workers are older women with a frail spouse or parent at home. A third challenge is the need for employee benefits that match the health and long-term care needs of an older work force. And yet another challenge is the intergenerational issue of equal rights for younger workers.

What I find troubling about these challenges is that social progress is usually slower and less productive, less predictive, and more frustrating than scientific progress. Health care is a classic example. At the same time that the United States brags about its contribution to modern science, we are still one of two

162

developed nations in the world without some form of national health plan. Employment is another humbling example; we continue to see problems of mandatory retirement, age discrimination, and inflexible benefit programs.

Although I seem to be painting a bleak picture, conferences such as this are a bright light for the citizens, the economies, and the social values of Japan and the United States. Our aging world may be the one challenge that brings developed and developing nations together through common scientific policy and human values. What more appropriate vehicle for peace is there than our concern for human rights?

Legislators, Backed by the People, Determine a Productive Aging Society

Ralph Regula

People need to know their U.S. Representatives, U.S. Senators, and state legislators. They need to share their ideas with us so that we, in turn, can develop responsible programs for the future. We should be listening to them instead of they to us. We set the parameters of these programs; we make the promises; we determine, in a sense, how long people are productive. We had the Pepper Bill in Congress last year, which extended the retirement age. And, of course, we have a great effect on the aging population because we deal with the program involving Medicare and Social Security.

Just what is the secret of old age? My grandmother lived with us for many years when I was a child. Whenever we had beef on the table (and that was quite often since I grew up in a farm family), she would always have everybody cut the fat off their piece and give it to her—she died at age 97. One can draw any conclusion he likes from this. I happen to be in the beef-raising business, so I have a prejudicial interest in that story. But that just illustrates how little we really know. Almost any day a person can pick up a magazine and discover that he can be on both sides of an issue.

We need, for example, to continually examine what is important to health. We have to make every effort to control costs,

164

while still giving quality service. Anyone who has any ideas on how people who want to stay home as long as possible can do so at less cost than being put into nursing homes should share these ideas with us.

The magnitude of the problem of aging was brought home recently at a meeting I had with the Cleveland Growth Association. In their packet of materials was a table indicating age groups for 1982, 1990, 2000, and 2010. For the year 2010, the percentage of those over 65 was much greater than it was in 1982 and, likewise, the percentage of small children was much less. This is significant, for it means that there's going to be a whole new set of challenges in the year 2010. We need to think about that because policies made on Capitol Hill will determine whether we can keep the promises we made to the aging. This, too, stresses the importance of people sharing with us their ideas on how this can best be done.

I just read where over the next several years the Social Security Trust Fund is going to grow by a great magnitude because we have a group that will be coming into its productive years. We're going to need every dollar in that trust fund. However, it's going to be a great temptation to all of us to say, "Well, the money's there, so we can give out a lot of benefits next year and the year after that because money will be flowing in." In so doing, we're going to deny the promise to those who are putting money in now and hope to draw it out in 2010 and 2020.

That's another example of how important it is that we keep our eye on the long term in this legislative arena, and how important it is that everyone share his or her ideas with us and support those who try to think in terms of the long-term future—not just next week, but in the next century.

The Aging Population:
A Global Issue

Larry Pressler

Japan and the United States have many similarities in their aging populations: Both countries are facing the fastest growth ever in their elderly population; both countries are struggling with how to best meet the needs of this growing segment of their society; and both nations want to build a mature, productive population.

As a member of both the Foreign Relations and Aging Committees of the U.S. Senate, I firmly believe we should work together and learn from each other's mistakes and successes. The aging of our population is not just a U.S. issue or a Japanese issue; it is truly a global issue. I had the privilege of being appointed by President Reagan as a U.S. Representative to the United Nations' Fall General Assembly in New York last year, and I believe that the U.N.'s World Health Organization is probably the best organization in which we can work together and share our experiences. Quite frankly, however, the goals of the Vienna International Plan of Action on Aging have not been carried out to the fullest. It seems that until the actual crisis occurs, such issues take a back seat.

This is unfortunate. There is widespread support for international cooperation on aging issues, but not a sense of urgency to accomplish the goals of the World Assembly on Aging. That is why we need conferences as well as organizations such as the Alliance for Aging Research.

"The Promise of Productive Aging" naturally brings to mind employment. While I voted for legislation extending the mandatory retirement here in the United States, I strongly believe that those who wish to retire should not be forced to continue to work. Employment is one option, but for many Americans, retirement is the option they have worked for and deserve. So as America, Japan, and the rest of the world continue to mature, we should do everything possible to ensure that both options are open. The choice is theirs. As a legislator, I have no right to dictate which avenue is the better one.

There are those of us in the United States Congress who recognize that how we prepare for and ultimately deal with the aging of our populations is one of the most critical questions of our time. I stand ready to help you in any way.

Health/Employment Policies and Later-Life Productivity

Claude Pepper

We need to work together to lay down conditions and provide policies under which our senior citizens may continue to play the vital and meaningful role that they played in earlier years.

The idea that we could lay down an arbitrary rule as to when people should stop working seems strange. Now it has become abhorrent to us to say by law to anybody in America who was doing a creditable job and performing honest work, "You have to stop because the Lord graced you with advanced age." You can imagine such a person saying, "What have I done?" Am I no longer functional, responsible, loyal, or competent because I have reached 65 years of age?" There was a presumption of disability under that law in this country. Except in a few limited cases, today there is no law under which anybody can be required to quit work simply because they have been blessed with advanced age. The elderly can look forward to the future with confidence, not fear.

Some elderly ask if they are standing in the path of the young. An older person has just as much right to work as a younger person. I do not know of any younger man who has the right to take my job just because he is younger than I. Of course, the answer is that we should provide enough jobs for both young and old. So the first thing that is important in showing a productive old age is to have no impediment in the way of the individual having a meaningful, constructive, and affirmative life.

Obviously, of course, there are two other things relevant to a productive old age. One is health. Generally, the elderly need about three times as much medical care as younger people, and so they should have access to whatever medical care they need. Congress is considering legislation that will make all needed health care available, with an individual paying what he or she can into a fund that would provide the care.

Additionally, older workers need to be given added confidence. Many who would rather not spend the last years of their lives continuing to do the same job should have instruction, training, and educational opportunities available to them that would either improve their skills in doing the work they are already doing or allow them to learn other skills. They should have an opportunity either to improve their existing skills so they can earn more or learn some different skill through additional training, in order to do something that they like to do. Retired or not, people who have spent many years wishing they had chosen something else as their life's work should have the opportunity of switching to a new activity that will be a joyous experience for them. People must be engaged in something that is so challenging and meaningful to them that they are delighted to have something to get up for in the morning. It is much better for most people to retire into some kind of active work rather than into just idleness.

Of course, there should be time for leisure. Many industries are giving people an opportunity of working part time, sometimes allowing two individuals to hold the same job. If one wants to go fishing, visit members of the family, or travel, the other one will carry on the work.

Work should not be an obsession or a burden but, rather, a pleasant experience, a productive endeavor, and a satisfying opportunity for the individual.

Legislative Changes
and the Elderly

Spark Matsunaga

As Chairman of the Subcommittee on Aging of the Senate Labor and Human Resources Committee, I am most interested in productive aging. Its policy implications are rising to the forefront of the national agenda here in the United States. Collaborative efforts between the United States and Japan can only benefit both of our countries.

As a nation, we Americans have been known to emphasize youth, but in recent years we have become increasingly aware of the implications of aging. Certainly there has been an ambiguity throughout human history with regard to a long life, and whether such an attainment represents a blessing or a curse hinges on matters of quality, notably with respect to health, self-esteem, and companionship. Productive aging is, of course, a matter of personal philosophy, but it must also be a matter of national philosophy. I firmly believe that the greatness of any nation can be accurately measured by the degree to which it cares for its elderly citizens.

We're all familiar with the demographic facts about the aging of the nation's population. The ranks of the elderly have grown more rapidly in this century than has the remainder of the population, and this trend is expected to continue into the 21st century. Between 1980 and 2020, the total population of the United

States is projected to increase by slightly more than 30%, while the 65-and-over population is expected to increase by more than 200%.

These startling demographic facts have caused some to predict growing intergenerational conflicts. Today, however, we have no strong evidence of such conflict within our graying America. A recently released survey prepared for the American Association of Retired Persons concludes that instead of discord, the generations share a mutual respect and a concern for one another's needs. The study further reports widespread rejection of an anti-elderly sentiment. It finds, for instance, that two out of every three Americans feel strongly that the older generation can continue to make important contributions. Significantly, only 13% believe that older workers should be encouraged to retire early in order to make room for the young. Moreover, there are no signs of waning support for programs targeted for the elderly. In fact, this study found younger Americans expressing deeper concern about the severity of the elderly's problems than do the elderly themselves.

It is against this demographic and social backdrop that the 100th Congress will be addressing many issues affecting the elderly, including catastrophic health care and the reauthorization of the Older Americans Act. The latter was a landmark piece of legislation when it was enacted in 1965. I'm proud that I was a co-sponsor of that measure. Through this legislation, Congress created a new federal program specifically designed to address social service needs. However, beyond the scope of the relatively small number of social service programs created at that time, Congress established the framework for a national policy on aging. The original act set forth 10 national policy objectives aimed at improving the quality of life of older Americans in the areas of income, health, housing, employment, retirement, and community services. Congress also created the Administration on Aging, which was directed to stimulate more effective use of existing resources for older persons.

As the act evolved through its successive reauthorizations and amendments, it has become the cornerstone for the development and delivery of a broad array of services for older persons. Major amendments in 1972 and 1973 created the National Nutrition Program for the elderly, and the National Network of Area Agencies on Aging. The 1973 amendments provided authority for the Community Service Employment Program for lower-income older persons under the auspices of the act. Subsequent amendments have expanded the authority and responsibilities of State Units on Aging and Area Agencies on Aging. During the 22 years since this enactment, the act has evolved from a program of small grants to one that now supports 57 state agencies and over 660 area agencies on aging. Annual appropriations have doubled.

In my capacity as Chairman of the Subcommittee on Aging, I have been conducting a series of hearings regarding the need for changes to this most important legislation. The first hearing addressed the changing needs of the elderly and focused on such issues as long-term care and assistance to special population subgroups such as the handicapped. The second hearing focused on the extent to which the needs of minority elders are being met through the Older Americans Act. Soon the subcommittee will discuss current services under the act, including nutritional programs, employment programs, and legal services.

Few issues touch upon all segments of our society as do those of an aging population. Whatever national policy emerges from the way in which our society comes to terms with its changing demographics, surely preserving the opportunity for a productive life will be one of the greatest contributions that can be made. Longevity provides the opportunity for our lives to come full circle, for there is no better recipe for youthfulness than useful activity. There is an ancient Japanese maxim that expresses this very well: "A soul completely immersed in one's work reflects a youthful face." As one of Japanese ancestry who learned this lesson from my father, I have put it to good practice; it seems to have worked on this 70-year-old senior citizen.

The New Problems of a New Aging Society

Orrin Hatch

Despite the miles that separate Japan and the United States and the differences in our languages, customs, and traditions, our two countries have much in common. It is common knowledge that we both love baseball, Sony walkmans, jeans, and sushi; however, it is not so widely recognized that we also share an almost obsessive fondness for numbers.

But when it comes to a true definition of "old," numbers can be misleading. Take, for example, my good friend and distinguished colleague Strom Thurmond of South Carolina. He is 84, and that number alone excludes him from 99% of the positions of responsibility and trust both here in the United States and in Japan. By the numbers, he should, by all rights, have retired years ago. But consider this: If there were 15 months in a year instead of 12, he would be only 60 which, indeed, is more like his true age.

Thus, "old" cannot be defined by a number. Any true definition must deal with individuals, not digits. It must include Benjamin Franklin, George Burns, Albert Schweitzer, Helen Hayes, Irving Berlin, Pablo Picasso, Ronald Reagan, and Akira Kurosawa. It must include our parents and grandparents, the 65-year-old widow down the block on Social Security, and the 85-year-old shut-in next door without it. It must include the healthy and the sick, the spry and the frail, the homeless and the homeowner. It must acknowledge the institutionalized, the deinstitutionalized, and the noninstitutionalized. It must take into account the cruelty of Alzheimer's and Parkinson's disease, the trauma of hip fracture and stroke, the loneliness from the loss of friends and loved ones, and the despair of long-ago-discarded dreams. And it must take into account where a person lives. In some societies 30 is old. In other parts of the globe, an 80-year-old is considered a young kid with a future.

Which brings us to another common denominator between our two countries: the aging of our populations. According to recent statistics, 12% of the U.S. population is 65 years or older; in Japan, it is 10%. By the year 2000, persons aged 65 and older are expected to represent 13% of the U.S. population and 15% of the Japanese population. By 2025, it will grow to 20% in the U.S. and 23% in Japan.

This seems to indicate a time for self-congratulation on our part that more people in our two populations are enjoying longer life spans and that statistics promise longer life spans to an even greater percent in the future. This is good news, indeed, but it also begets new problems we need to deal with: catastrophic illness, long-term care, community care, transportation, bioethical questions about dying, abuse of the elderly, and special diseases of the aging.

Dealing successfully with the problem of medical services for the elderly alone seems almost insurmountable. Here in America, Medicare does not cover what many older people need most: long-term care. Although 80% of American elderly will never have to be in a nursing home, every family is anxious, asking themselves who will take care of their grandparents/parents should they suffer, for example, from a stroke or hip fracture.

No policy issue is more central than catastrophic health care protection. The fundamental question that Congress has to quickly decide is what kind of care can be offered and where that care should be provided. Examples of financial ruin caused by catastrophic health care costs can be found in every state. Roughly 9 million elderly Americans suffer from chronic heart or lung conditions; 4 million suffer from Alzheimer's disease; many elderly have severe problems due to stroke. The result, in many cases, is financial disaster for the victims and their families.

The Reagan administration has proposed a plan that focuses on the hospitalization and doctors' fees caused by catastrophic illness. For an additional premium of $4.92 per month, Medicare pays for unlimited hospitalization. Patients pay no more than $2,000 in out-of-pocket expenses.

This is a start, but much more is needed. The real financial disaster for many older Americans is not hospitalization but long-term care at home or in nursing homes. The latter alone costs an average of $22,000 a year in the United States. Currently, most is not covered under Medicare. This is why I continually work on passage of Home Health Care legislation.

I will introduce several Home Health Care bills during this session of Congress. One will double the personal exemption for families who care for an aged family member needing medical support. A second bill authorizes a demonstration project to look for new ways to pay for Home Health Care through the savings that it generates. A third reauthorizes the Homemaker/ Home Aid training grant program, which provides funding for local educational training programs. Yet another provides $100 million for states to provide health care services in the homes of the chronically ill, reimbursing for a professional health care team to help in the home.

I have also been concentrating on biomedical research, an important and appropriate role for a federal government. For example, when I was chairman of the Senate Labor and Human Resources Committee, I fought for reauthorization of the National Institutes of Health, a federally funded agency whose mission is to conduct and support biomedical research into the causes, prevention, and cure of diseases.

This legislation, the Health Research Extension Act of 1985, represented a milestone in public health policy here in America. It created the National Institute of Arthritis, Musculoskeletal and Skin Disease, and the National Center for Nursing. It reauthorized the "war on cancer" by strengthening provisions of the National Cancer Act of 1970 and included special provisions on health and lung diseases. All in all, it ensured that the United States could maintain an active presence in the world's medical health research.

If our two nations are to shape policy intelligently, we need to share data—demographic and social, economic and physical.

Social and Personal Planning for Productive Aging

John Glenn

Aging is one thing; *productive* aging is something else. The United States and Japan share a common interest in giving people an opportunity to live healthier and fuller lives.

The demographic projections for the year 2000 tell us that sooner or later virtually every nation will have a population that is increasingly older. Now is the time to plan for a future that will bring new challenges and new opportunities as we deal with older populations. For once, can't we in government—here and around the world—foresee a problem and address it in advance, not just wait for the wreck to happen and then try to pick up the pieces, making do with stopgap, Band-Aid measures? Knowing that this is coming, can't we for once take advantage of that lead time to do something about it?

The fact that I'm no longer Chairman of the Special Committee on Aging does not lessen my interest and activity in it. My interest in problems and opportunities in aging returned some years ago. My wife, Annie, had been asked to be the honorary chairperson of the Ohio Nursing Home Week. She spent that week going around Ohio checking into some of the nursing homes, actually staying the entire night in some of them to see what it was like. In fact, she saw fit to extend her trip for another week because she was so interested in it. Out of that and our

177

previous interest came my volunteering, after arriving in the Senate, to serve on the Special Committee on Aging. It was not something I was assigned to do; it was something I wanted to do.

Pursuant to those interests back home in Ohio, I held a series of hearings on women in our aging society. We addressed some of the important changes that are reshaping American society and opening gaps between our current policies and our future needs. We discussed what should be done today to ensure healthy and independent lives for our future generations of older Americans, particularly older women. Although the problems associated with aging obviously affect men as well as women, we put special emphasis on women for one very simple reason: In the United States and, indeed, throughout the world, women outlive men. I don't like to admit that, but it's true. So the problems of aging may be more often the problems of women, but all of us, especially those with Y chromosomes, hope that survival rates for men will improve substantially in the years ahead.

In the meantime, we must pay special attention to how today's life expectancy gap affects our planning. Overcoming chronic diseases and the disability and fear they cause among older Americans must be a top priority in our efforts to improve the quality of life for older Americans here and also in other nations. To that end, I will continue to oppose the Administration's proposals to reduce federal funding for biomedical research, and I am proud to join Senator Sasser in introducing legislation to establish Centers of Excellence in Geriatric Research and Training at medical schools throughout the country.

More government spending isn't the only answer; given our federal budget deficit, we simply cannot afford unlimited spending. Fortunately, there is a growing body of evidence that health promotion measures can significantly reduce the chance of developing chronic illness—in other words, preventive medicine. We apply preventive maintenance to machines; we do it to trucks; we do it to all sorts of devices because we know it makes them last longer. It's no less true for our human bodies. We can significantly reduce our chances of developing chronic illness if we provide preventive maintenance programs. The truly good news is that we're never too old to start. A sensible diet, an end to smoking, and a good exercise program can help even those over 65 live healthier and happier lives.

I hate to stress the number 65, for as of my last birthday, I'm now in that age group. When you go by that magic 65th birthday, you do start thinking seriously about self-help. I didn't think I'd pay that much attention to it, but every time I now get an ache and pain, I think maybe I'm further over the hill than I thought. Thus, these days I'm seeing self-help as the most important tool we have in combating chronic illness. We need to increase our efforts to educate people of all ages about the benefits of life-style changes.

Another important aspect of an improved old age, important both to individuals and to society, is the ability and opportunity to continue to be productive. We do not need to be "ware-housed," put away somewhere because we are getting older. To meet that challenge requires the combined efforts of govern-ment, the private sector, and individuals. Congress has passed legislation intended to keep people working past the so-called normal retirement age of 65. Normal retirement age varies from one nation to another. Japan's retirement age is 60, compared with our 65. The United States has eliminated mandatory retire-ment for most workers, required continued pension accruals for workers over 65, liberalized the social security earnings test, and scheduled a rise in the social security retirement age to 67 in the next century. Along with the private sector, we are attempt-ing to provide training and retraining for middle-aged and older workers and develop policies that may better accommodate them, such as flex-time and job sharing.

However, the trend toward early retirement continues. This causes serious concerns about the economic status of the elderly who are living more years in retirement, as well as concerns about the shortages of skilled labor in certain industries. At a time when increasing numbers of Americans are healthier, bet-ter educated, and living longer, this early-retirement trend just doesn't make much sense.

To help reverse it, we need accurate information about the changes that occur when we age and about the tools that are available to assess a person's ability to perform a particular job, regardless of chronological age. Assessing the capabilities of older workers will aid in understanding just how their skills can best be utilized. These are just a few of the things we can expect from research into the underlying biological mechanisms of normal aging processes. Particularly important are longitudinal studies designed to distinguish normal aging from the effects of disease.

In 1980, Dr. Butler, then Director of the National Institute on Aging, joined me in addressing these issues at a hearing I chaired on "How Old is Old? The Effects of Aging on Learning and Working." In 1985, Dr. Butler arranged a hearing called "The Greying of Nations," held at Mount Sinai during the 13th International Congress of Gerontology. There we heard from 12 leading geriatricians and gerontologists from around the world about the importance of coordinating our research efforts on a global basis. One scientist, from the Soviet Union, had gone into areas where abnormally large numbers of people aged 100 and older live. He testified that their longevity is not completely attributable to their eating a little bit of yogurt, as our TV ads of a few years ago wanted us to believe. It appears that the very orderly life, the very routine existence, may have a bigger effect than almost anything else. In fact, genes, which we don't completely understand yet, may play an even larger role.

At that hearing, people from all over the world shared their knowledge about aging. Such collaboration will help explain the aging process and accelerate the transmission of scientific information into actual practice. In this way, we can improve the provision of health care and social services; we can educate all members of society, including older people themselves, about the physical and mental capabilities of the elderly, thus eliminating myths and stereotypes that lead to age discrimination and unproductive lives.

As is becoming more and more common, I've had several careers during my own working life: as a military man, an astronaut, a businessman, and a United States senator. My wife sometimes tells me that she thinks having so many careers shows that I could not hold a steady job, but I don't necessarily agree. By standard definition, I became a senior citizen on my last birthday. That doesn't mean I feel that old. Just because I hit 65 does not mean I'm going to stretch out and await the Grim Reaper or the call of the Lord; I plan to be productive, and that's the important thing.

We want to keep on being as productive as we possibly can, and the opportunity to do so is a promise that must be made and kept for all people today. As we plan ahead for our growing elderly population of the 21st century, we must all employ our skills, our knowledge, our power, and our wealth to help people everywhere lead happier, healthier, more meaningful lives for as many years as we're privileged to walk upon this earth. Although we may not be able to do anything to avoid getting older, we can do a great deal to ensure that we're getting better.

The Political Clout of Aging Americans

John Melcher

Our country has about 28 million older Americans, slightly more than those aged 20 or younger. This number will grow during the next 50 years to about 30 to 35 million. I look at productive aging from the older American's angle; I hope others do, too. In Congress—both in the Special Committee on Aging and on the Senate floor—I view these older Americans as my best friends.

For older Americans, health care needs are a high priority because of the costs of hospitals, physicians, medication, home health care, and that dreaded end result for a million-and-a-half Americans: nursing homes. Older Americans have a great deal of political clout and have learned that there is no party line on these issues. Among all Americans, no age group votes as consistently and turns out as heavily at elections. They may be slowed down in many ways, they may have health problems, their activities may be slower, and they may sleep or rest longer. But whatever their physical infirmities, they have 20/20 vision politically. Thus, their political significance is a very real phenomenon that will continue to be more influential and more important. I applaud my best friends' growing political clout.

The Focus: "Care"
More Than "Cure"

Claudine Schneider

The Japanese have the world's highest life expectancy: 80 years for women. Seeing as my agenda for aging is 130, I wonder if I should be spending more of my time in Japan to pick up on some of those secrets. The average age for Japanese men is 75. By contrast, American women are expected to live to 78 and men to 71, so there's not too much disparity there. But I think that as we are recognizing that our population is becoming more and more aged, and there are constant references to the aging of America, we have to also recognize that progress in research on the aging process and in making for a more productive life for the aging is going at a slow pace.

As I am a member of both the House Science and Technology Committee and the Aging Committee, it has come to my attention that right now 73% of our federal research budget is being dedicated to defense-oriented research. We need to contrast that with the 8% that will be used to fund health research, which, I am sad to report, is down from two years ago when it was 10%. We will spend $67 million this year to research Alzheimer's disease, which will afflict at least 7 million Americans by the year 2040. By contrast, we spent $1.8 billion over the past 10 years to develop the Sergeant York gun. I'm sad to report that the York gun did not work and, as a result, that money went down the drain.

Our priorities for spending for health care services are way off base, with our focus on cure rather than care. Medicare, for example, will finance high-cost, high-tech procedures, but it will not provide the reimbursement for many routine diagnostic procedures. Medicare will not pay for annual checkups, nor for cancer screening such as mammograms, nor for nutritional counseling to minimize the risk of heart disease and stroke.

Considering that I intend to live to be 130—and I intend to do that in good health—I'm picking up a little bit of my own technique. I had read that psychoneuroimmunology is something we ought to be paying close attention to. I happen to practice that each morning and night. Whether it works or not, only time will tell, but quite frankly, I am a strong supporter of increased investigation into prevention not only for care but also for cure.

Thus, I think all these areas need to receive adequate emphasis. In whatever part I can play, being a member of the Science and Technology Committee and the Aging Committee and one who is very much interested in the graying of America, my support can be counted on.

Setting the Agenda for the 21st Century   12

INTRODUCTION TO CHAPTER 12

This chapter brings together the ideas of two men, inveterate volunteers, in their 80s: Ryoichi Sasakawa and Arthur Flemming. Both personify and advocate productive aging. Mr. Sasakawa expresses productive aging through his international philanthropies, including contributions to the eradication of smallpox and assistance to people with leprosy. In a message read by Dr. Kenzo Kiikuni of the Sasakawa Memorial Health Foundation, Mr. Sasakawa talks about sharing his good health with people whose lives are blunted without access to needed scientific technology.

Mr. Flemming, a former U.S. commissioner of aging (Nixon Administration) and a former Secretary of Health, Education, and Welfare (Eisenhower Administration), focuses on older people as an untapped community resource. Distressed that some elders turn passive upon retirement, he argues for investment in recruiting and training them for careers in productive volunteering.

Amplifying these themes, foundation executive Thomas Moloney asserts that elder productivity is essential to the United States, which mindlessly has "sent an entire generation of productive people off to play golf." The 21st century can be one of reemploying elders. In particular, he sees future grandparents uniquely able to assist young families in the emotional and moral development of children.

What roles may elders play as industry increasingly applies automation? Osamu Nishio, a tool manufacturer, brought a philosophical rather than an economic outlook to the conference. Asserting that people rather than machines are the real producers, he finds that automation requires competent human supervision. The wisdom and competence of elders are needed for spiritual and intellectual as well as material progress, he says, drawing on American thinking.

Frameworks for planning in an aging society are emphasized by Daniel Schulder of the National Council on the Aging. Mr. Schulder considers how a longer working life can be planned for, especially the need for flexible retirement and disability-accommodating employment systems. An example of incomplete planning in the American social security system is the scheduled rise in the age of retirement with full benefits—to gradually reach 67 in the year 2027. The change makes no sense without (1) policies to extend the working life (e.g., incentives and job opportunities) and (2) provisions for individuals whose retirement before 67 for reasons of poor health and hazardous work will mean reduced benefits. No such policies were considered by Congress when enacting the age change.

For Herbert Gleason, an attorney and health policy specialist, institutional adaptations for productive aging must extend to the funding of health maintenance services over the entire life span. He believes these services should be available as a universal entitlement.

Perhaps Mr. Moloney voiced most succinctly the bedrock view of the conferees by saying that the elderly "may not need us, but we certainly need them."

The Elderly: An Untapped Community Resource

Arthur S. Flemming

I recently overheard a conversation in a church. Some people approached an older couple and asked if they would accept a particular assignment. The elderly couple's response was, "We've done that. Let the younger people pick it up." Just yesterday I participated in a nationwide TV call-in program. Someone called in to comment, "I have many opportunities for older persons to become involved as volunteers, but they do not seem to want to respond." We must change the prevalent attitudes of older persons toward volunteerism by developing positive recruiting programs that contribute significantly to our nation's productivity. Community service organizations could utilize the services of many volunteers, and older persons could respond to that need constructively. They represent an untapped resource.

If we are going to tap that resource, we must invest in counseling programs that help older persons figure out how they can match their training and experience with volunteer opportunities. Some people think that if an older person wants to work as a volunteer, all he or she has to do is go out and work as one; that is not the case. Just as we need to invest in counseling persons about their first careers, we need to invest in counseling persons who are thinking about a second or third career. As a result, the older person will focus on a particular opportunity and recognize that she or he may need to participate in a short-term training program—a program that should be available.

Such programs should point out to the older person that working as a volunteer is a challenging assignment, one that draws on his or her experience and training and yields the psychological compensation that comes to those who know they are doing things that help others achieve their highest potential. We have increasing numbers of persons aging productively, but we can add to those numbers considerably if we develop positive programs designed to recruit older volunteers.

The "Reemployment" of the Elderly

Thomas W. Moloney

The elderly may get along without productive aging, but the country can't get along without the elderly aging productively. In other words, they may not need us, but we certainly need them. They may not need us because they may choose to do whatever they want to do. Guaranteed incomes and numerous health care choices allow them to physically and socially isolate themselves from other generations if they wish to do so. But they need to make other choices for the future health of the American economy and the American family.

With so few people over 65 working and so many in their early 60s retiring, we now have the largest number of the healthiest and best-educated group of adults not working in the history of any country at any time. How did this happen? Simply because we told them we didn't need them. As late as the 1970s, we believed that America's competitive edge in technology had such an inalienable lead that we would remain a world economic leader, while we sent an entire generation of productive people off to play golf. Second, the largest generation in history, the baby boomers, wanted their jobs. We didn't seem to have the time to figure out how to employ both generations, so we took the easy way out and simply retired the former. Third, we set up the Social Security and tax systems so that the correct economic decision for a person over 60 was to retire and run. Fourth, as a result, the elderly's status became centered on leisure, rather than employment or even social contributions.

There is great optimism for great change in the 21st century. We can reverse this trend if we make it clear to the elderly that we can't do it without them. First, I believe that their productive capacity is crucial to the highly competitive international economy that the country now addresses. We simply can't hope to maintain our standard of living if the largest and best-educated generation is asked to be parked on the sidelines. Secondly, we're not going to have another generation of baby boomers breathing down the current baby boomers' necks, for the "baby bust" is coming. We must take the time to figure out how to employ two generations productively. Third, we have to adjust the Social Security and pension systems further so there are real incentives for remaining in the work force. If this is done, status will also change.

Currently, thousands of Florida's elderly who literally don't need the income are finding satisfaction and new status in returning to the work force. It's reasonable to expect that nonemployment among the elderly has bottomed out and that the 21st century will be the century of reemployment of the elderly. With any encouragement at all, today's percentage of working people 65 to 70 can move from a little less than a quarter to better than a half by the 21st century, and those working people 70 to 75 can move from a little less than today's one in six to one in three. If this happens, the whole country will be significantly better off.

Then, too, we must consider the elderly's role in the future of the American family. Today's parents alone don't have the time to see to the intellectual, moral, emotional, and physical development of their children. The future consequences of this are absolutely staggering. The biggest single solution is not day care but, rather, the engagement of grandparents in the development of their grandchildren, a new 21st-century extended family. We can't buy moral and emotional development of children, but we may be able to obtain it through the grandparents. We must reverse the current perception that "hands off" is the best inter-generational policy.

Why is "hands off" the perception today and what might be done to change it? Part of the answer is in the difference in the formative life events between grandmothers today and those women who will be grandmothers in the next century. Inter-viewing today's grandmothers reveals two startling things. One stems from the fact that their own parents were indeed a burden —people in poor health, with low incomes, and often without housing. Their own parents took a good deal of their incomes, moved back in with them, and required a lot of care. Thus, the first thing today's grandparents say is, "I don't want to be a burden to my children." Secondly, since the careers of grand-mothers today were largely based upon raising their children, at a considerable cost of doing other things, their second message is something like, "I raised my children; they ought to raise theirs." Thus, their primary goal is to do no harm to their chil-dren's families and basically stay out of the way.

The formative events of grandmothers of the next century are nearly the opposite. First of all, their own parents haven't been a burden: They haven't had to pay their income, for Social Secu-rity's done that; they haven't moved back in with them, for their parents have maintained their own housing, even as widows liv-ing alone. They correctly see the grandparents of their children as healthy, independent people with money—not as a great bur-den, but as a great resource. Secondly, these are women who didn't have an enormous amount of time to spend with their own children and now look forward to giving more time to their grandchildren. Their formative events may take them to a posi-tion that says: "Don't stay out of the way but get involved. Be a resource; relieve the pressure your own daughters feel that you once felt yourselves."

If this is to happen, the 21st century may be the beginning of a new family phenomenon, whereby grandparents have the re-sources, time, experience, and patience to emerge as major factors in the development of their grandchildren in a society where parents will continue to be unavailable for the highly labor-intensive process of child rearing. Let's tell the elderly how much their productive aging is going to mean to the rest of us. Let's let them know that both our future standard of living and the intellectual and moral fiber of our children depend enormously upon their participation. And when they do come through for us, I just hope we're smart enough to give them the status and recognition they'll deserve.

Automation and Generational Continuity

Osamu Nishio

I have not yet found a ready-made answer to the problem of how man can successfully manage human interaction with automation. When automating production facilities, we must be sensitive to the interaction between man and machine.

Automation aims at maximum cost efficiency and, ultimately, elimination of human input. To attain this, a computerized control system, robotics, and artificial intelligence may be employed. Although this emphasis on efficiency and economic merit seems to imply that workers have no role in modernizing industrial technology, this is far from the truth. Automation improves the production process, and producing goods more rapidly and less expensively does require man's input.

The first step in automation, mechanizing the production system, involves substituting human energy with machine-produced energy. However, one should not hastily conclude that this initial phase totally eliminates man's work. In fact, in designing an automation system, the cooperation of machine operators is indispensable. Operators must tell the engineer which work process needs changing in order to improve efficiency. A competent engineer must then be able to suggest various ideas on how to deal with those problems.

Additionally, engineers who operate a production system

must constantly deal with discrepancies between designed and actual machine performance. A blueprint may not work if it does not consider aspects of the real world; a machine may not operate as expected. Such discrepancies require adjustments in closing the numerous gaps between design and actual performance.

Automation is most successful when engineers and operators work closely together in attempting to understand any problems that might arise. They must share problems and exchange opinions freely in order to create a consensus and mobilize a concerted effort at implementation.

Ultimately, it is human beings, not machines, who produce. Well-equipped plant facilities are fine, but what is really needed for successful automation is competent human performance. To do so, human beings must continue to learn. An ancient philosopher summarized it succinctly: "If you cultivate yourself in your middle age, you will not decline in your old age. If you cultivate yourself in old age, your accomplishments survive even your death." Men and women on the shop floor must learn to use their skills well and transmit them to the next generation of workers. Without generational continuity in technology, we cannot advance automation successfully.

In closing, I would like to make mention of a book I came across 15 years ago, David Lilienthal's *TVA, Democracy on the March*. The author observes that machines may largely replace physical labor, but they do not free men's minds; modern technology helps man to be productive, but it does not necessarily enrich human life. Man is responsible for finding freedom and happiness. In short, fruitful interaction between man and the machine requires wisdom, openness, experience, and self-cultivation.

Planning a Longer Working Life for an Aging Society

Daniel J. Schulder

Our society must be conscious, not afraid, of the impending heavy investments in planning and designing ways to discover, rediscover, invent, and adapt useful and productive roles for older citizens now and in the future. We who seek to expand the productive roles of the elderly should pay close attention to certain factors. For example, do we have any kind of an agreeable plan to accomplish the goals stated in this conference? Planning can reasonably maximize the positive results.

We lack a national organizational framework and public and private policy mechanism through which we can express our concerns and effectively make contributions toward a better and age-irrelevant society. Today, it's difficult to cite any significant public policy that will enhance our abilities to design and expand future employment roles for older adults. The one significant overriding policy is the delay built into the Social Security Act so that one will have to be 67 by the year 2027 to collect full benefits. Unfortunately, Congress, in its wisdom to secure funds for Social Security, did not provide any significant positive incentives for workers to stay in the work force, but did provide severe penalties.

First, things such as pension portability should be included in our planning. Second, lifelong training and upgrading should be

195

an entitlement for all workers. This could include one or more sabbaticals for workers at all levels and in all trades, which might be paid by modified pension or Social Security benefits at the choice of the worker. A 60-year-old with the wherewithal to pursue an associate degree as an environmental technician makes good economic sense. If he can get a job in solid waste disposal at age 62, we can expect 10 or more years of stable employment from him, more than we can expect of the worker coming into the same kind of job at the age of 22 or 23. It's significant that in most defense-related technical organizations today, if you are an engineer but not a manager at age 45, your chance for six months off to hone your skills are practically nil; however, two years later, at 47, you're up for a pay increase, but you don't get it because they'll say, "He didn't keep up with technical developments in his craft."

Third, we need to change our concepts of vocational rehabilitative medicine and services to emphasize capacities, not impairments, of older workers and then, through a thorough functional assessment system of the jobs and of the workers, match these to the actual performance standards to be filled—in other words, emphasize capability and not limitations.

Fourth, we need to change our pension and Social Security systems. Rather than require an all-at-once decision to get out of the work force, we should experiment with partial retirement entitlements, proven so effective by many other countries in keeping people in the work force well into their 70s.

In short, we need to have a plan to take out some of the rigidities of our employment and retirement systems. If we don't, we face a noble but frustrating future. Additionally, we should carefully examine the full implications for older workers of the growing information industry. The information explosion in work and in communications is contributing to the undermining of corporate hierarchy, changing the nature and competition of jobs, promoting public and private decision making by participatory consensus making and not by command structures alone. It's estimated that by the year 2000, fully 60% of all jobs in this country will be directly related to the "knowledge industry." The social and economic brews being stirred by technology, trade, demography, and advocates for more equitable training and income systems for persons of all ages may have unparalleled opportunities in the next decade to construct new and exciting work and volunteer opportunities, especially for our aging work force.

When American industry really stops pushing older workers out with bogus early retirement schemes and provides true job and career mobility for workers of all ages, we will know that we are all better prepared for the full contribution to national productivity that older workers will make in the 21st century.

Health Maintenance Services: A Universal Entitlement

Herbert Gleason

One word, "Productivity," is the catalyst that explains so much about what our approach to and the possibilities of aging can be. There have been achievements: Medicare and the elimination of mandatory retirement age. But we have so much further to go. We have to eliminate the disincentives for earned income under Social Security. What an outrage that you lose your Social Security when earning money, but not when just sitting back and collecting dividends. There is something obscene about that. It is so counterproductive to what we should be advancing in this country.

If we're going to have any impact in the next century, we need to immediately address the health agenda—and I emphasize health, not medical, agenda, for there is a difference. Health, productivity, and age are inseparable. We are what we do. If we believe there is something significant in what we do, our lives are meaningful. If we compared the health status of what we call "unretired" people with the status of those who don't perceive themselves as usefully employed, I'm sure the results would reveal a noticeable difference in morbidity.

Of course, I don't mean remunerated employment. There are so many activities that need to be done in our society that we could place dignity on, communicate prestige to, volunteerism, for example—caring for relatives, friends, and children, without having to be rewarded with money. One of the most rejuvenating activities for the elderly is observable in movements like the Grey Panthers, where older people are engaged in setting their own agenda and in mobilizing their immense political power, as well as working to improve the health care system.

Three points need to be made about the health agenda. As noted previously, the distinction between health and medicine is important, for we're always confusing it, using misnomers. We talk about health care when we mean medical care; we talk about health insurance when we mean sickness insurance; we talk about life insurance when we mean death insurance because we're so squeamish about telling the truth. The answers for the elderly do not primarily lie in medical care, even for their health status. Yet everything we're significantly doing in the expenditure of public and private funds supports the medical delivery system and not the health delivery system. What the Reagan Administration has pitifully advanced is a program for catastrophic intervention for very ill, very old people. That isn't health care, and to call it the catastrophic proposal is a catastrophe. What it will mean is more of the same pathological orientation that we have seen over the years for Medicare, where everything has to be done in a hospital because the only place you get paid for doing it is in a hospital. If people are going to be paid only for catastrophic illness, then we're going to see a lot more health catastrophes before people can be helped.

Secondly, the answer to a more sensible approach to health care delivery lies in the HMO mechanism, and yet all our policies have diminished its effectiveness.

Finally, whenever confronted with a choice in health or medical policy, try to apply the test of universal entitlement. We are hung up on addressing ourselves to particular segments of the population that need special intervention, but we cannot design a public policy for a nation by looking at individual cases. To be sure, we must not ever overlook the individual, but we must have a policy that works for everybody; then we can look and see how it applies to each individual.

Afterword

A basic premise of the concept of productive aging may be stated as follows: There is a vital connection between health and productivity. In other words, when we are productive, we preserve our health; when we are healthy, we are likely to be productive. This is an important point for each of us personally, as well as for society as a whole.

Many other important thoughts about productive aging emerged from the symposium. In discussing the notion of productivity, one of our contributors pointed out that any talk about work should also include talk about love. Work and love are the two life-enhancing and affirming aspects of human existence.

We learned that there is very little evidence for a serious conflict among the generations, and, in fact, much evidence testifies to the contrary. Most polls reflect a deep affection and concern of the young for the old and, conversely, the old for the young.

Some of the contributors questioned the idea of a fixed box of resources and goods, that is, that we are somehow operating under a "zero-sum game." Despite the reality of the federal deficit, it seems clear that we must undertake new social initiatives now, or else, as many speakers pointed out, "pay later." We must begin to shift priorities and make new statements on the social matters we consider important, statements that express basic values about the human condition and the course of human life.

This will require a shift in thinking away from past concentration on cost to a focus on opportunities for young and old to continue being productive. For example, what may be seen as costs from one perspective can be seen as jobs if looked at from another perspective. A perfect illustration of this is the U.S. health industry. We often hear of the tremendous cost burden of this industry. Yet we rarely hear that it is the second largest provider of jobs in the nation and the second largest contributor to the gross national product.

The importance of aging research was stressed by many of our contributors. Bringing an end to Alzheimer's disease is just one example of the benefits such research can bring. The association of aging with senility and debility has been rampant in both Western and Eastern civilizations, but when Alzheimer's disease is eliminated, we will probably see a very different imagery of old age.

Although productivity was our main focus in the symposium and this book, we need to emphasize as well individual entrepreneurial activity and creative human imagination, without which we really cannot sustain the longevous populations of Japan and the United States. Both Japan and the United States will have to face still another serious problem: the understandable and naturally occurring aspirations of the developing world. It is time to start thinking about how we can protect the jobs, health, and welfare of our two nations' citizens while assisting these developing nations.

Where do we go from here? There is surely no shortage of work to be done, on an individual and collective basis. Surveys reveal that people underestimate the amount of time they have left in life. How can we build an individual life plan if we're not more conscious of the fact that we're going to live longer? This is not to counsel morbid preoccupation with the problems of age or longevity but, rather, to suggest that we do have a personal and collective responsibility to plan for our future and the opportunities that a longer life can bring.

Many specific problems were identified by our contributors, and there are many things to consider doing in response. For our part, the organizers of the "Promise of Productive Aging" symposium are planning future contact between our two nations' scholars and scientists, including collaboration and exchange. We plan to look for models of productive aging among individuals, families, communities, and work arrangements. Promoting communication among policymakers and scientists in Japan and the United States will help lead us more surely and quickly to a better and more productive old age.

ROBERT N. BUTLER

Appendix A

Japan Shipbuilding Industry Foundation,
Tokyo, Japan

Ryoichi Sasakawa, Japan's pre-eminent philanthropist, is Chairman of the Japan Shipbuilding Industry Foundation, which he established in 1962. A former member of Japan's House of Representatives, Mr. Sasakawa helped revitalize his nation's merchant shipping industry following World War II. He founded Japan's motorboat racing industry in the first decade after the war and directed proceeds to the Japan Shipbuilding Industry Foundation, which, in turn, has funded numerous charitable projects in Japan and around the world. In recent years, the foundation has distributed substantial amounts outside Japan for disease prevention, disaster relief, education, social welfare, and family planning programs. Through contributions to the World Health Organization of the United Nations, Mr. Sasakawa is credited with a leading role in the eradication of smallpox and efforts to wipe out leprosy in the Third World. On three occasions, his work has been recognized by the United Nations, including the UN Peace Prize in 1982. Mr. Sasakawa's contributions have also been recognized with the Martin Luther King Peace Prize, the Linus Pauling Award for Humanitarianism, and the Helen Keller International Award.

Alliance for Aging Research, Washington, D.C.

The Alliance for Aging Research is a private, nonprofit, bipartisan advocacy organization working to promote gerontology and preventive geriatrics in the national interest. The Alliance strives to broaden the public discussion of the "Graying of America" to include scientific research that could lead to healthy, vigorous, productive old age for a greater number of people. Sponsors of the Alliance for Aging Research are the Commonwealth Fund of New York, the John D. and Catherine T. MacArthur Foundation, Retirement Research Foundation, Transamerica Life Companies, ARCO, David L. Brown, Chairman of Telescan, Inc., the Equitable, Hoffmann-LaRoche, Inc., Merck & Co., Sandoz Pharmaceuticals Corp., and the Travelers Insurance Companies.

Gerald and May Ellen Ritter Department of Geriatrics and Adult Development, The Mount Sinai School of Medicine, New York City

The Gerald and May Ellen Ritter Department of Geriatrics and Adult Development, founded in 1982 at the Mount Sinai School of Medicine, is the nation's first medical school department of geriatrics. It was established as a response to the growing need for physicians trained in the principles and practice of geriatric medicine in order to care for the projected rapid increase in the older population. With its outstanding academic program of teaching and research and comprehensive services for older persons and their families, the Ritter Department's overall goal is to assist all contemporary medicine in developing and applying the skills, knowledge, and attitudes that will ease the impact of the demographic revolution.

Appendix B

THE AGING IN AMERICA[1]

- Twenty-nine million Americans—12% of the population—are 65 and older.

- Fifty-one million Americans—21% of the population—are 55 and older.

- By the year 2000, nearly 34 million Americans will exceed age 65 and comprise 25% of the population.

- By the year 2000, some 54 million people will be 55 and older.

- In 1985, there were 2.3 million people 85 and older.

- Americans 85 and older represent the fastest growing segment of the population. This group is expected to triple by 2020.

- American women over 65 outnumber men by 100 to 67.

- Only 5% of those 65 and over live in institutions; one in four of those is 85 or older.

- Life expectancy for American women is 78 and 71 for men.

AGING IN JAPAN[2]

- Nearly 12 million Japanese—almost 10%—are 65 and older.

- By the year 2000, more than 20 million Japanese—almost 16%—will be 65 and older.

- The ratio of Japan's elderly population to its total will exceed that of the United States by 1990.

[1] 1980–1985 estimates by the U.S. Bureau of the Census.
[2] Official Japanese statistics from the Government of Japan Report.

- In 1983, there were more than 450,000 Japanese 85 and older.

- Japanese women over 65 outnumber men by 100 to 72.

- More than 900,000 elderly women live alone in Japan.

- In 1985, life expectancy in Japan is estimated to be 80 years for women and almost 75 years for men.

INCOME OF OLDER AMERICANS

- Median income for families with a head of household who is 65 and older is $18,215.

- Median income for unrelated individuals—as opposed to couples —is $7,296.

- Median income for all individuals 65 and older is $13,460.

- Median income for those aged 65 to 69 is $16,420.

- Median income for those aged 70 to 74 is $13,600.

- Median income for those 75 to 79 is $11,810.

- Median income for those aged 80 and older is $10,810.

INCOME OF OLDER JAPANESE

- More than one-half of Japan's elderly live on pensions.

- The largest group of Japanese elderly live on less than 100,000 yen—approximately $650.00 (February 1987) per month.

EMPLOYMENT OF OLDER AMERICANS[3]

- Twelve million—54% of Americans—aged 55 to 64 are employed.

- Almost 3 million—11% of Americans—65 and older are employed.

---

[3] Bureau of Labor Statistics.

- More than 1 million—7% of Americans—aged 70 and older are employed.

EMPLOYMENT OF OLDER JAPANESE

- One out of every four—or 26%—of those 65 and older is employed.
- In 1982, more than 640,000 unemployed older people wanted jobs—half of them to increase income.

Name Index

Subject Index

215